Also by Ethel Johnston Phelps

TATTERHOOD AND OTHER TALES

THE MAID OF THE NORTH

FEMINIST
FOLK TALES
FROM AROUND
THE WORLD

ETHEL JOHNSTON PHELPS

ILLUSTRATIONS BY

LLOYD BLOOM

An Owl Book

Henry Holt and Company • New York

Henry Holt and Company, Inc.
Publishers since 1866
115 West 18th Street
New York, New York 10011

Henry Holt® is a registered trademark
of Henry Holt and Company, Inc.

Published in Canada by Fitzhenry & Whiteside Ltd.,
195 Allstate Parkway, Markham, Ontario L3R 4T8.

Library of Congress Cataloging-in-Publication Data
Phelps, Ethel Johnston.
The Maid of the North.
Bibliography: p.
1. Heroines—Fiction.   2. Tales.   I. Title.
PS3566.H38M3   813'.54   80-21500

ISBN 0-8050-0679-6 (An Owl Book: pbk.)

Henry Holt books are available for special promotions
and premiums. For details contact: Director, Special Markets.

First published in hardcover in 1981 by
Holt, Rinehart and Winston.

First Owl Book Edition—1982

Designed by Joy Chu

Printed in the United States of America
All first editions are printed on acid-free paper.∞

15   17   19   20   18   16   14

TO CAROL LEVIN AND

RANICE CROSBY

for more reasons than I could ever list

CONTENTS

• • •

Contents

INTRODUCTION

• • •

$\mathcal{T}$he traditional folk and fairy tales in this collection, as in my earlier book of tales, have one characteristic in common: they all portray spirited, courageous heroines. Although a great number of fairy and folk tale collections are in print, this type of heroine is surprisingly rare.

Taken as a whole, the body of traditional fairy/folk tales (the two terms have become almost interchangeable) is very heavily weighted with heroes, and most of the "heroines" we do encounter are far from heroic. Always endowed with beauty—and it often appears that beauty is their only reason for being in the tale—they conform in many ways to the sentimental ideal of women in the nineteenth century. They are good, obedient, meek, submissive to authority, and naturally inferior to the heroes. They sometimes suffer cruelties, but are patient under ill-treatment. In most cases they are docile or helpless when confronted with danger or a difficult situation.

In short, as heroines, they do not inspire or delight, but tend to bore the reader. I think it is their meekness that repels. They are acted upon by people or events in the tale; they rarely initiate their own action to change matters. (In contrast to this type of heroine, when clever or strong women appear in folk tales, they are usually portrayed as unpleasant, if not evil, characters—cruel witches, jealous stepmothers, or old hags.) It is not my intention to delve into the psychological or social meanings behind the various images of heroines in folk tales, but simply to note that the vast majority are not particularly satisfying to readers today.

In actual fact, the women of much earlier centuries, particularly rural women, were strong, capable, and resourceful in a positive way as hard-working members of a family, or as widows on their own. Few folk tales reflect these qualities. Inevitably the question arises: How many, if any, folk tales of strong, capable heroines exist in the printed sources available?

In a sense, this book grew out of that question. Over a period of three years I read thousands of fairy and folk tales in a search for tales of clever, resourceful heroines; tales in which equally courageous heroines and heroes cooperated in their adventures; tales of likeable heroines who had the spirit to take action; tales that were, in themselves, strong or appealing.

As a result of that search, the heroines in this book are quite different from the usual folk and fairy tale heroines. In a few of the tales, the girls and women possess the power (or knowledge) of magic, which they use to rescue the heroes from disaster. The hero may be more physically active in the story, but he needs the powers of the self-reliant, independent heroine to save him.

In the majority of the tales, the heroines are resourceful girls and women who take action to solve a problem posed by the plot. Often they use cleverness or shrewd common sense. Duffy outwits the devil; a Zuni maiden breaks a hunting taboo; a clever monkey outwits a shark; an old Japanese woman escapes from the Oni; Mulha tricks an ogre to save her sisters.

All the heroines have self-confidence and a clear sense of their own worth. They possess courage, moral or physical; they do not meekly accept but seek to solve the dilemmas they face. The majority have leading roles in the story. However, the few who have minor roles (in terms of space) play a crucial part in the story and have an independent strength that is characteristic of all the heroines here.

Although most of the printed sources for the tales I've chosen are from the nineteenth century, the tales themselves are part of an oral, primarily rural, tradition of storytelling that stretches far back into time. Each generation shaped the tales according to the values of the times, adding or subtracting details according to the tellers' own sense of story. While the characters and basic story remained the same, it was this personal shaping of the tales that may explain the many variations of each story that now exist. As every folk tale reader knows, different versions of the tales are found in different countries and even on different continents. Variants of Cinderella and of tales of hero/heroines bewitched into nonhuman form are particularly widespread.

The twenty-one folk tales retold here come from many countries; approximately seventeen different ethnic cultures are represented. However, while samples of clever heroine tales can be found on almost every continent, there are proportionately more strong heroines (in the published tales available) from northern Europe and Britain. Undoubtedly many factors are involved, including cultural attitudes toward women; perhaps the more rugged life of early people in colder climates made strong, resourceful women valuable as marriage partners. At any rate, in the present volume, the larger number of tales from this area reflects this availability of sources.

In giving the older tales of our heritage a fresh retelling for this generation of readers, I have exercised the traditional storyteller's privilege. I have shaped each tale, sometimes adding or omitting details, to reflect my sense of what makes it a satisfying tale. The stories of Maria Morevna, the Maid of the North, and "Finn Magic," for example, have been compressed to make a smoother flow of narrative.

Most of the tales in this book follow the story outlines of earlier sources quite closely. In a few cases I've added my own details to amplify the story's ending, as in "The Giant's Daughter," "The Husband Who Stayed at Home," and "Elsa and the Evil Wizard."

The tale "Fair Exchange" is retold with the most freedom. Of the many tales of changelings in Celtic folklore, none caught my imagination for retelling. The story of the lass in "Fair Exchange" springs from a brief incident in one of Lady Wilde's tales of Irish folklore. I developed the incident of the girl who confronted the Fairy Queen to get her own child back into the present story, blending elements of other folk tales to fill in the details.

For two of the tales ("Gawain and the Lady Ragnell" and "Lanval and the Lady Triamor") I have used as sources the versions of fourteenth-century literary storytellers who drew on oral folk tales of their period. As might be expected, these are more complex than other tales in the collection. However, there are tales to appeal to the very young as well as the more sophisticated reader. Through the tales' diversity, the reader becomes aware of the extraordinary vitality of the folk and fairy tale heritage, not only in the range of imaginative fantasy but also in humor.

I confess a partiality for the lighthearted tale. The humor here is most obvious in the comic tales of "Duffy and the Devil," from

Cornwall, and "The Husband Who Stayed at Home." There is sly humor in the chaos caused by the powerful Gina in "The Giant's Daughter." In the Punjab story of the clever wife, "The Tiger and the Jackal," it is the two animals who provide the humor. A sense of the comic pervades "The Monkey's Heart," where a small monkey uses her wit to get rid of a shark, and "Elsa and the Evil Wizard," where the enraged wizard is defeated by a young girl. Even "The Maid of the North," a tale from the heroic saga known as the *Kalevala*, contains a clear thread of skeptical humor.

Four of the tales in the book deserve longer comment. The tale of Lanval dates back to the twelfth century, if not earlier, and has many variants. Fairy women who marry or mate with humans are found frequently in Celtic folk tales. They are powerful, independent women who confer benefits on the man of their choice; the terms they state for the union always contain a taboo, and always they glow with the radiant, eternal youth of the Other World.

This is the one tale in the present collection where dazzling beauty is a plot element—but it is the humans who place false value on the illusion of beauty, not Triamor herself. It is clear that Triamor's dazzling beauty is a supernatural attribute. The ability of fairy folk to create an illusion of glamour was well known to the Celtic peoples who told and listened to these tales. Actually, Triamor's strange beauty is a side issue; the mainspring of the story is Triamor's power to confer fame and wealth. She grants young Lanval his heart's desire and adds the usual taboo to their pact—in this case, Lanval is forbidden to mention Triamor to humans.

The tale is a little more complex than most folk tales using this basic plot. As usual, the human's impulsive thoughtlessness causes the breakup of the pact and the withdrawal of good fortune. In this tale, Triamor relents at the end and rescues Lanval—if dwelling in the shadowy Other World of fairy folk can be called a rescue. Implicit in the tale is a moral concerning Lanval's fate. Extravagance and thoughtless speech brought about his first misfortunes. Although Triamor rescued him from that state with her magic bounty, this good fortune was again lost through thoughtless speech—a character flaw that may seem minor to us. Nonetheless, Lanval did achieve his dream of wealth and fame for a time, and his departure for the Other World of fairy folk may not be a sad fate after all.

The basic fairy tale plot of "Gawain and the Lady Ragnell" was old in Chaucer's day (as the Wife of Bath remarked when she told a variant of the tale). By the late fourteenth century the tale had become attached to King Arthur and Gawain, in the sense that they were given the leading male roles in the story. Of all the northern tales told about Arthur and Gawain, this one is the tenderest and most appealing. It will be noticed that the King Arthur and Gawain of northern British folklore are quite different from the same characters in White's *The Once and Future King* or Malory's *Le Morte d'Arthur*, drawn from French sources. To the storytellers in the north of Britain, Gawain was the ideal of a hero, Arthur was flawed with human failings, and Lancelot was a minor knight rarely mentioned. The northern tales of Arthur lack the high romance of the French tales, but their dry humor and ironic realism are very engaging.

This is a tale of shape-changing and evil enchantment. Ragnell faces her terrible situation with courage, saves Arthur's life, and finds in Gawain a man with the necessary personal qualities to help her break the enchantment.

The underlying theme, a woman's right to freedom of will and choice, weaves the different story elements together. The woman who "wanted her own way" was often made fun of in folk tales, for it is an issue as old as human relationships. It's refreshing to find that a few tales do handle the theme in positive terms—and delightful to find the theme used as a basis for a romantic story.

Like the tale of Gawain and Ragnell, "Finn Magic" is told from the hero's point of view. Although there is no doubt that Zilla is a heroine of strength and courage, hers is a much smaller, though crucial, role. However, the theme of ethnic prejudice is unusual; I felt that the story belonged in this collection, despite the fact that Zilla is seen only through Eilert's eyes. Whatever her role may be in rescuing Eilert from the Draug and Merfolk (the tale is deliberately discreet on this point), it is clear the Nordlanders believed she possessed magic spells or influence over the people beneath the sea. While Eilert may be uncertain about Zilla's magic, he does recognize her physical courage in saving him.

"The Maid of the North," the longest story in the book, is drawn from the Finnish saga, the *Kalevala*. Kalevala is known as the Land of Heroes, and the saga deals primarily with the heroes' adventures, feuds, and journeys to the North Land. However, woven through the songs and tales in the saga like a bright thread is the story of the Maid and her mother, Louhi. I have pulled out the incidents dealing with the Maid of the North in order to tell her story as a separate tale.

All the women in the *Kalevala* have strong, independent characters. This particular tale is concerned with Louhi, the ruler of the North Land, and her daughter, the Maid—who, as is often the case in folk tales, is not given a specific name. Although the women and the heroes in the tale have supernatural powers, these powers are limited; they often land in predicaments from which their powers cannot extricate them.

The heroes from Kalevala have magic in powerful word and song charms; the two women from the North Land have lesser and quite different powers of magic. Both the heroes and the women rely on guile rather than physical force. Although in this retelling it was necessary to compress the heroes' adventures, they are without doubt the most energetic characters in the tale, and the women from the North Land regard them with mocking amusement.

Of the three very different heroes who seek to marry the Maid, she finally chooses young Seppo the smith. Given three impossible tasks to perform, Seppo turns to the Maid for help; the Maid's clever counsel enables him to accomplish the "impossible" and saves his life.

The charm of the tale lies in the humorous vitality of the characters. Despite their prodigious deeds and powers, the heroes (in fact, all the characters) are engagingly human in their frailties.

Although I have taken the greater part of this introduction to speak of the remarkably spirited heroines I have culled from the large body of traditional folk tales, I cannot end without a few words about the heroes who appear in some of the tales with them. By and large, they are not the stereotyped heroes of most fairy and folk tales. They are not flat cardboard characters, but are individually appealing in their own right: Eilert, who struggles with family loyalty before breaking through prejudice; Prince Wilhelm in despair over dual promises; brave Alexey, who redeems his mistake of impulsive curiosity; extravagant and thoughtless Lanval; the compassionate, incomparable Gawain; and the shy master smith, Seppo, who wins the heart of the Maid of the North.

But enough has been said about the quite special heroines—and heroes—in these tales. The proof is in the reading.

THE MAID OF
THE NORTH

A Finnish Tale from the Kalevala

· · ·

Long, long ago Finland was called Kalevala, the
Land of Heroes, for the people who lived there possessed magic in
the power of words. They could sing a word spell strong enough to
heal mortal wounds, raise a golden pine tree, or even challenge the
power of Hiisi the Evil One. In the cold, snowy land to the north
dwelt a very different folk, and the most powerful of these were the
Mistress of the North Country, old Louhi, and her daughter, the
Maid of the North.

Early one morning, after Louhi's farmhouse had been swept and
scoured, a young serving girl came out into the yard to empty a pan
of scraps. Hearing a strange sound from across the river, she stopped
to listen, then ran back into the house.

"Someone is in trouble across the river, Mistress," she cried. "It sounds like a child weeping."

Old Louhi came out and crossed the yard to peer through the gates. On the distant, marshy shore of the river, she could barely make out the form of a man, but she could clearly hear his despairing laments. "That's not a child weeping," she remarked. "It's more likely the wild moaning of a hero in trouble!"

Louhi hurried down to untie the boat moored at the river's edge. Then she rowed across the wide river to the place on the bleak shore where a gray-bearded man was standing.

"Who are you, stranger?" called Louhi as she came near to him. "Where do you come from?"

"I come from the south—from Kalevala, the Land of Heroes, and I am a great man in my own country," he answered. "But I've met with terrible misfortune, and now I'm completely lost in this strange, bleak country." He added bitterly, "I should have stayed at home!"

"Come out of that soggy marsh and get into my boat," said Louhi briskly. "I'll bring you back to my farmstead, and you can tell me all about your troubles."

The shivering old man climbed gratefully into the boat. Louhi, with strong strokes of the oars, sent the small craft skimming back across the river. Then she fed him, warmed him before the fire, and dried his wet clothes.

"I am Vainamoinen," he said when he was dry and comfortable. "In Kalevala, I am known as a singer of powerful songs."

Louhi nodded. She had heard of Vainamoinen and his powers of magic. "And what brings you to the North, Vaina? Why did you leave the rich green fields and sunny lakes of the South?"

He sighed. "I am a foolish old man. I decided it was time I was married, and I thought to find a wife in the North Country." Then he related the troubles and misfortunes that had befallen him on his way north. "And finally," he concluded, "when I was thrown into the sea, I swam desperately for days until an eagle from Lapland took pity on me, swooped down, and carried me off on his back. He dropped me there on the marsh." He shivered. "It is a cold, gloomy country. I want nothing more than to leave it and return to my own land."

Louhi regarded him thoughtfully. He was, she knew, a magician of great power—deposited, so to speak, on her own doorstep. It was possible he could be of use to her.

"Stop your lamenting, Vaina," she said kindly. "You have come to a good country. You could live here in comfort. There is honey mead to drink, plenty of salmon on the table, and pork—"

"I don't care for strange food in strange houses," he said crossly. "A man is better off at home, where his power and dignity are known. I am too old to search for a wife."

"If that's the case," said Louhi craftily, "what will you give me if I send you back to the green fields of your own land?"

"Whatever you like!" said old Vaina eagerly. "A hat full of silver and gold? Two hats full?"

"Gold and silver are not of much use to me," said Louhi, "and I have copper in the Copper Mountain yonder. But life is not very easy here in the cold North Land. The one thing I want is a magic Sampo—a mill that grinds out flour and meal on one side, salt on the other, and coins on the third side. If you could make me a magic Sampo, I'd give you a horse and sledge to carry you home in comfort!"

When Vainamoinen did not answer, Louhi went on, "I have the white swan's plume needed for its making, but where is the hero who can forge the Sampo?"

Vaina knew he had no power to forge a Sampo. He said cautiously, "I've heard of such a thing, but nothing like that exists in all the land."

"I have a handsome daughter, the Maid of the North," Louhi added slyly. "I will give my daughter in marriage to whoever will make me a magic Sampo."

Vaina's eyes lit up for a moment. Then he said regretfully, "I cannot make you a Sampo. But I do know a man who can—Seppo Ilmarinen the Master Smith. He is the greatest smith in the Land of Heroes. It was he who forged the dome of the sky. You see how smooth it is—not a hammer mark on it! If you send me back to my own country, I promise that Ilmarinen will come to the North Land to forge you the magic Sampo."

"Agreed," said Louhi. She thought that Ilmarinen would be just the man for the work. She harnessed a horse to the sledge, settled fur rugs around old Vaina, and gave him cold salmon and eggs for provisions.

"The horse will take you south swiftly and safely. He knows the way. But I have one word of warning for you," said Louhi. "Do not lift your head to look upward or around you until you arrive in Kalevala. If you do, misfortune will follow."

Vaina thanked her for her kindness and drove off. His head sunk in thought, he considered how he was going to persuade his friend Ilmarinen to go to the North Country.

Vainamoinen had traveled only a short distance on his journey when he heard a sharp, clicking clatter of sound. What could it be? He looked about him. There was nothing in sight but snow and distant forests of pine and spruce. Forgetting Louhi's warning, he lifted his head and looked upward.

He stared in amazement. Quite close above him in the gray northern sky was the arc of a rainbow. On the rainbow sat a dazzling young woman weaving at a loom. There was only one young woman who could sit on a rainbow—with a loom or without—and that was powerful old Louhi's daughter, the Maid of the North.

"So this is why the old sorceress forbade me to lift my head!" thought Vaina. "She did not want me to elope with the Maid of the North before she gets her Sampo!"

The girl on the rainbow was laughing at him. Vaina remembered he had been seeking a wife, and he thought this dark-haired charmer would do very well.

"Climb down, Maid of the North, and sit beside me in the sledge," he called.

"Why should I do that?" she asked in amusement.

"I will take you home with me to the fair South Land. You can bake bread for me, brew my beer, and talk to me gaily when I come home in the evenings."

Her laughter rang out. "Yesterday I heard a bird singing of marriage. I asked him if a woman was happier in her own house or in the home of a husband. Do you know what he answered? 'A maiden's lot is brighter than a day in summer, but a married woman's lot is colder than frost. A girl at home is as free as a berry in a garden, but a wife is like a house dog tied with a rope.' Why should I be a servant and wait upon a husband?"

"The bird knows nothing about it!" Vaina answered irritably. "Every girl should get married! I will not make a bad husband. I am no lazier than other heroes."

The Maid laughed again at Vaina's words. "I'll think about it—if you will split a horsehair with a knife and tie an egg into knots without breaking the egg!" she mocked.

Vaina smiled and climbed out of the sledge. "That's nothing for a hero from Kalevala!" He plucked a hair from the horse's mane. Taking a knife from his belt, he split the hair cleanly into pieces so thin one could scarcely see them. Then he took an egg Louhi had given him and tied it into knots without even cracking the shell.

"Now will you come and sit in the sledge with me?" he called.

"Perhaps," said the Maid. "Let me see you peel a stone and chop a block of ice without scattering any chips."

Vaina peeled a stone as neatly as an apple and chopped the ice fine, without spilling a chip.

"There!" said Vaina, very pleased with himself. "Now will you come down to the sledge?"

"Very clever," admitted the Maid. Then, with a grin of mischief, she said, "I might come down if you make me a boat from the wooden pieces of my loom, and if you launch the boat without touching it!" She tossed the loom down to him and sat back to watch.

"There is no man in the world who can build boats better than I can!" boasted Vaina. Taking his ax from the sledge, he set to work. Hour after hour he worked—until a downward blow of the ax slipped and cut deep into his knee. He hopped about in agony, the blood gushing from the wound. Too late, he remembered Louhi's warning of misfortune. He looked upward, but both the Maid and the rainbow had vanished.

He sang all the healing spells he could think of; he gathered moss and lichen for poultices, but nothing stopped the flow of blood. He had once known of a special magic spell for cuts from iron, but in his anger and frustration he could not remember it.

There was nothing to do but climb into the sledge and rush off to the next village for help.

"Is there anyone here who can heal the wounds of iron?" he shouted as he drove through the village. Only one old man answered yes. With his mighty word spell, the old man stopped the bleeding, then called for his son to bind Vainamoinen's knee.

Limping back to his sledge, Vaina drove on south. He thought that perhaps the Maid was not a suitable wife for him after all.

. . .

Louhi was not very pleased when she learned how her daughter had amused herself with Vainamoinen.

"You should not have offered me for a Sampo!" answered the Maid. "You know I don't want to be married—and certainly not to an old man!"

"It was just a manner of speaking," said Louhi. "I meant I would not oppose the match. You could do worse, my girl!" Louhi went on, "You should treat Vaina with more respect. He's the greatest magician in the South, and he's promised to send us a master smith to forge a magic Sampo. How else would we get a Sampo?"

"I think Vaina will forget all about it once he is in his homeland," answered the Maid scornfully.

"No," said Louhi. "He will keep his promise to send the smith."

But Vainamoinen was not at all sure he *could* keep his promise. Suppose Ilmarinen did not want to go to the North Land? Thinking it was best to be prepared before he saw his friend Ilmarinen, he went to the edge of a grain field near his home and began to sing a magic song. As he sang, a great pine tree with golden needles grew before him, reaching high into the sky. He sang a shining moon onto the very top, and the stars of the Great Bear onto the upper branches.

Well pleased with his work, he went off to the smithy where Ilmarinen the Sky Maker wielded his mighty hammer.

"Where have you been all this while?" asked the young smith.

"I've been to the North Land," said Vaina. "You should visit the North Country, Seppo. It's a wonderful place!"

"Not from what I've heard," his friend retorted. "I've heard tales about the North Land. It's said the people there eat each other and drown heroes! It's not a place I'd want to visit!"

"Ah, but Seppo, the girls there!" Vaina said slyly. "You need a wife, and the Maid of the North is a charming, delightful girl. Beautiful dark hair and dark eyes—quite different from the fair-haired girls here."

"I'm not ready to marry," said Seppo, "and I'm not particularly interested in girls. So why should I go to that cold, bleak country?" He laid down his hammer. "What's behind all this, Vaina?"

"Old Louhi will give her daughter, the Maid of the North, to whoever makes her a magic Sampo," said Vaina.

"How does that concern you? I'm the only one who could make a magic Sampo," Ilmarinen said slowly. "What have you done? Promised Louhi I would make it?"

Vainamoinen turned red. "It's a mere trifle for a great smith like you. But truly, Seppo, it's a strange, marvelous country. Come see what I've brought back from the North—a pine tree with needles of gold, and the moon and the stars in its branches."

"I don't believe it! There's nothing in the North but snow and ice."

"Forget about the Sampo and the Maid. I can see you're not interested in marriage or in going to the North Land. But come with me and I'll show you one of the wonders of the North."

The smith followed Vaina to the edge of the field. There indeed stood the pine tree Vaina had described!

"You think it is only an illusion? Climb up into the pine tree and touch one of the stars," said Vaina complacently.

Now, Ilmarinen was the greatest master smith in Kalevala, but he was a simple, straightforward young man, easily beguiled. He began to climb the pine tree.

As soon as Seppo neared the upper branches, Vainamoinen began to sing up a storm. The wind rose, and lashed wildly through the branches. Then, at Vaina's command, the wind bore Seppo Ilmarinen off through the air, high above the forests and lakes, to deposit him right inside old Louhi's front gate.

When Seppo looked around him, he knew he was in the North Land in spite of himself. His old friend Vaina had tricked him.

Old Louhi hurried out of the house to greet the stranger. "Where are you from, stranger? How did you get here? The watchdogs did not bark!"

"The way I came, a watchdog would be afraid to bark!" answered Seppo, still resentful.

Louhi looked puzzled. "Oh? Never mind, come in. You're welcome at our table."

The farm was much larger and more comfortable than Seppo had expected in the North Land, and the dinner set before him was not one he could complain about, either. When a tall, dark-haired girl with sparkling eyes and a merry smile came into the room, his interest was caught at once.

"Ah!" said the Maid. "I see we have another hero from the South."

"My daughter has many suitors," said Louhi hastily. "Tell me, young man, have you ever heard of Ilmarinen the great smith and master craftsman? We have been expecting him. He is to make me a magic Sampo."

"I am Ilmarinen the Master Smith, sometimes called Seppo by my friends," he answered.

"So you are Ilmarinen! Can you forge a magic Sampo for us?"

"It was I who hammered out the vault of the heavens," he answered simply.

"A Sampo should be an easy thing for a craftsman like you to make!" Noting the way he gazed at her daughter, Louhi added slyly, "In return, would you like this charming girl for a bride?"

Ilmarinen had been thinking old Vaina had not done him such

an ill turn after all, in sending him to the North Land. Vaina was right—the Maid was a delightful girl.

"I will make you the magic Sampo," said Seppo. "Where is your smithy?"

Louhi had to admit there was neither furnace nor forge—nor bellows, nor hammer and anvil. All these would have to be made first, before Ilmarinen could forge a magic Sampo. This was discouraging, but Seppo told himself cheerfully, "Heroes never despair!"

Louhi willingly supplied men to help him build the smithy and to work the bellows once the forge was completed. But even with the forge made, the work of making the Sampo went slowly.

At last, after many trials and errors, a splendid magic Sampo, with a top of many colors, was finished. When pressure was applied to a lever, the Sampo ground out flour meal from one side, salt from another, and coins from the third side. After it had ground out several barrels full of flour, salt, and coins, Louhi had it carried to the Copper Mountain and secured with locks. It was her most valuable treasure, and she didn't intend to have it stolen.

Ilmarinen, weary and black with soot, took a bath in the sauna. Then he presented himself to Louhi.

"Mistress Louhi, I have made the magic Sampo for you. May I have your daughter for my wife?"

Before Louhi could think of an evasive answer, the Maid of the North said, "Did you think I would leave the pine forests and sweet meadows of the North Land, where I can hear the cuckoos and the bluebirds sing in summer? Where I can roam at will to gather flowers and berries? Why should I go off to a strange land with a husband? No, thank you! I do not intend to marry so soon!"

Ilmarinen stared unhappily at the floor. So much for Louhi's fine offer! He had fallen in love with the Maid. Now he realized sadly that she would not leave the carefree life of her mother's farm to become a wife. He would have to return home without her.

Louhi bustled about to set a rich feast before him. Then she gave him a boat with a copper paddle and called the north wind to blow him safely home. On the third day he was home in his own smithy.

He was building a fire in his cold furnace when old Vaina showed up.

"Well, Seppo? Did you make the magic Sampo for Mistress Louhi?"

"Yes, I forged it," said Ilmarinen with a sigh. "Much good it did me! The Maid of the North refused to have me for a husband."

"Never mind," said old Vaina, quite relieved at this news. "There are plenty of fair-haired girls here in Kalevala who will be glad to marry you."

"I'm not interested," muttered Ilmarinen.

Vaina went away feeling rather pleased. "So the Maid refused handsome young Seppo!" he said to himself. "I wonder if she still thinks of me? Perhaps she is sorry she teased the oldest, most powerful magician in Kalevala!" Still dazzled by the vision of the laughing Maid of the North seated on a rainbow, old Vaina decided he would not give up the idea of marrying her. She had asked for a boat from the wood of her loom, he remembered. Very well, he would build a mighty boat, the most splendid boat ever made, and sail back with it to the North Country.

. . .

While Vaina was felling great oaks for his boat, another hero arrived at Louhi's farm. He was the vain dandy Kauko, called Lemminkainen, the Great Lover. Although he believed all the girls in Kalevala were charmed by him, he thought the girls of the South much too giddy. He had already gotten rid of one wife because she would not sit quietly at home as he demanded.

"I am Kauko Lemminkainen, the great singer of songs, and I

come from the Land of Heroes," he announced. "I know more magic songs and spells than anyone in the North Land."

"Indeed!" said Louhi. "And what is that to us?" She looked him over, not liking what she saw—a rude fellow, too full of his own importance.

"I've come to marry your daughter, the Maid of the North," he told her. "Where is she?"

"Marry the Maid? Not likely!" she scoffed. "Whatever put that idea into your head?"

"It's said in Kalevala that the Maid of the North refused old Vaina and young Seppo. And who can blame her? A charmer like that is the wife for Lemminkainen!"

"You'd have to go out and capture the Great Elk of Hiisi the Evil One before I'd even consider such a match!" This was Louhi's sharp way of saying no, for to capture the Elk of Hiisi the Evil One was an almost impossible task. Many heroes had tried it.

Lemminkainen smiled in a superior way, put on his skis, and strapped a pack on his back. "I am a mighty hunter. There's not a four-footed creature in the land that can escape me," he boasted. And Hiisi the Evil One heard his boast.

The Maid of the North came outside with Louhi to watch Lemminkainen disappear into the distance.

"I hope you don't fancy that one for a husband," said Louhi.

"Not at all!" said the Maid. "Why should I want to marry a noisy little rooster like that?"

Lemminkainen chased the Great Elk of Hiisi day and night, uphill, downhill. He glided along with amazing speed until he chased the Great Elk to the far end of the North Country and came up at last beside the creature. He threw his lasso over its head, tamed the Elk with words, and dragged it back to Louhi's farm.

"Mistress, I've caught the Elk of Hiisi for you," said Lemminkainen. "Now give me the Maid."

"Not so fast!" cried Louhi, thinking quickly of another way to get rid of him. "You must bridle and bring back the Wild Horse of Hiisi for me."

"That shouldn't be too difficult," said he. Strapping on his skis, off he went with a bridle of silver cleverly worked with gold. Again he traveled swiftly over the cold North Land day and night until he came upon the Evil One's Wild Horse. The mighty stallion was a terrifying sight. His mane was a mass of fiery flames, and a cloud of smoke poured from his nostrils.

But Lemminkainen, with powerful word spells, put out the flames. Once the flames were gone, the stallion was tame. It was quite easy to put on the bridle of gold and silver and ride the horse back to Louhi.

When Louhi saw him ride into the farmyard on Hiisi's Wild Horse, she thought with irritation, "These heroes from Kalevala with their magic of word spells! But I won't have this arrogant fellow wooing the Maid."

"Well, Mistress!" cried Lemminkainen triumphantly. "Here's the Horse of Hiisi. Now the Maid—"

"I can see that you're a proper hero!" said Louhi. She went on craftily, "I said I'd consider your offer, and I will. There's one last thing you must do—you must shoot the White Swan of Tuonela with a single arrow."

This was the most dangerous of the tasks she had set, for the White Swan lived on the river of Tuoni, the Lord of the Dead. Many heroes had sought the White Swan and never returned.

Taking his bow and quiver of arrows, Lemminkainen set off confidently for the dark lands of Tuoni. When he at last found the river, running black through the dark rocks and caverns in the Land of the Dead, he stood uncertainly on the bank. He peered through the gloom, waiting for a sight of the White Swan.

But Hiisi the Evil One now took his revenge. From the dark,

tumbled rocks on the bank, Hiisi loosed a poisonous serpent who sank his fangs into Lemminkainen's heart. The young hunter crumpled to the ground, dead.

And that would have been the end of Lemminkainen, had not his mother possessed considerable magic power of her own. Far away in Kalevala, she knew at once that evil had befallen her son. Journeying to the far North and on into the dreadful lands of Tuoni, she found her son's body where it had fallen.

Her word charms had no effect. Her son lay still and cold. Summoning a bee, she bade her fly to the fields of Ukko, the Creator of Life, and bring back honey from his fields. The bee flew off at once and returned with the precious drops of life. These she rubbed all over her son's body.

"Wake from this sleep of evil dreams," she sang. "Rise, my son, and leave this wicked place."

Lemminkainen stretched and woke. "I have slept a long time."

"You would have slept forever if it hadn't been for me," said his mother.

He looked into the dark gloom around them. "Where am I?"

"You're in Tuonela, and the faster we leave here, the better," said his mother briskly.

"But I must shoot the White Swan of Tuonela if I'm to win the Maid of the North," he cried.

His mother looked at him with exasperation. "You don't realize the narrow escape you've had! Let the Swan alone and forget the Maid of the North. She's not for you. Come along back to Kalevala with me and choose a girl of your own kind."

For once Lemminkainen took his mother's advice. He returned to the South, and Louhi and the Maid were well pleased to be rid of him.

. . .

By this time old Vaina had finished his boat. It was without doubt the finest, strongest boat in Kalevala. He had painted it red and decorated the prow and sides with gold. Then, early one morning, he brought provisions aboard and hoisted a red and blue sail.

Early as it was, Annikki, Ilmarinen's sister, was up even earlier, washing clothes at the edge of the shore.

"Where are you going, Vaina?" she called.

"Salmon fishing. The salmon trout are spawning."

"Don't tell me a silly lie," said Annikki. "You have no nets or tackle. And besides it's not the season."

"I'm going after wild geese," said Vaina impatiently.

"Another lie!" she laughed. "You have no bow or hunting dogs. Tell me honestly where you are going, Vaina."

"Well," said the old magician, "I did lie a little. Actually I'm going off to the cold and misty North Land."

When Annikki heard this, she dropped her washing and ran as fast as she could to the smithy.

"Seppo!" she called to her brother.

He laid down his hammer. "What is it?"

"I have interesting news for you. And I think I deserve earrings and a ring for bringing it to you!"

"I'll make you the trinkets if the news is important," said Seppo.

"Are you still thinking of that girl up in the North Land?" Of course, Annikki knew very well that Seppo was still brooding over the tall, dark-haired Maid. "Do you still want to marry her?"

Seppo stared at her. "And if I do?"

"Well, you've done nothing about it! While you are here working your head off at the forge, crafty old Vaina has just set sail for the North Land."

It took Ilmarinen only a few moments to realize what this meant. "I'm going on a journey. Get the bathhouse ready for me, Annikki. I'll need a steam bath to wash off this soot. Kindle a fire of chips, get the stones hot, and bring plenty of soap. While you're doing that, I'll gladly make you the ring and earrings!"

Annikki hurried to gather firewood for the sauna. When at last she came to tell her brother the bathhouse was ready, he had made her not only a ring and earrings, but a slender silver girdle as well.

Ilmarinen rubbed and scrubbed and steamed himself until his skin and hair were shining. He dressed carefully in a fine linen shirt, trousers, and stockings his mother had woven. He pulled on smooth leather boots. Then he put on a blue coat lined with red, and over that a furred, heavy wool cape. His sister handed him warm gloves, and his mother gave him a handsome fur hat his father had worn as a bridegroom. Dressed at last, the tall, powerful Ilmarinen looked very splendid indeed.

While the horse was being harnessed to the sledge and his gear packed, Ilmarinen had a servant fetch six golden cuckoos to sit on the frame and seven singing bluebirds to perch on the reins. Thick furs were brought for him to sit on, and to cover him against the northern cold.

Cracking his whip, he drove off along the shore at a steady pace until, on the third day, he overtook his old friend Vainamoinen, sailing out on the waters.

"Vaina!" he called. "Let's make a friendly agreement so there'll be no hard feelings. Let us agree the Maid shall choose freely and fairly between us."

"I agree to that," answered Vaina. He was sure the Maid would choose himself, the wise, old magician, the greatest singer among the heroes. Nonetheless, he got out the oars and rowed to help speed the boat along.

Not long after this, the yard dogs at Louhi's farm began to bark furiously. Louhi sent the serving maid out to see who approached.

"Strangers coming," she reported when she returned to the house. "Someone in a sledge and another rowing a red boat."

Louhi had the serving maid put a new log on the fire. "If the log sweats blood, the strangers bring trouble," said Louhi. "If it sweats water, they come in peace."

They all watched the log intently. But it sweated neither blood nor water. The new log oozed honey. Louhi tasted a drop to be sure. "This means the strangers are noble suitors!" she exclaimed.

She hurried out to the gates to see for herself. Now the red boat with the elegant gold swirls on the prow was pulling to the shore. Handling the oars was the gray-haired, gray-bearded hero, Vainamoinen. The sledge drew near, gay with singing birds perched on the reins. She saw with misgiving that the splendidly dressed driver was Ilmarinen, the smith who had forged her magic Sampo.

"Those two heroes from the South are here again," said old Louhi as she came back into the house. "Vainamoinen brings great treasure in his boat, I'll wager. The young Seppo brings nothing but his fine clothes and singing birds!"

"Singing birds?" The Maid began to smile. "Are they cuckoos and bluebirds?" She ran to the door to look for Seppo's sledge.

Louhi called her back impatiently. "It's time you made up your mind about marriage. You'll have to choose between them. I advise you to draw a cup of mead and offer it to the man of your choice."

The Maid was silent.

"I leave it to you to choose," her mother went on briskly, "but if you have an ounce of sense, you'll take my advice and choose old Vaina. He's the wisest and most powerful of all the heroes—and besides, he's loaded with treasure."

"I'm not interested in money or treasure, nor in the power of an old man. When I marry, it will be a strong young man," said the Maid stubbornly. "Ilmarinen is a master craftsman. He may not be as wise or as powerful with word spells as old Vaina—but he did make the magic Sampo!"

"Don't be foolish," said old Louhi sharply, for she had made up her mind she would like to have the great magician Vainamoinen for her son-in-law. "If you marry a smith, he'll be covered with sweat and soot most of the time. Think of all that washing—you'll spend every day scrubbing the soot from his clothes!"

"I don't care about that," said the Maid.

Just then, Vaina entered the house. "Fair Maid of the North," he said politely, "will you marry me? Remember, you asked me once to make a boat from your loom? I did have a little trouble with that. But now I have made a magnificent boat, strong enough to sail the seas and weather every tempest."

"I don't care for sailors," said the Maid coolly. "Marry a man who thinks so much of boats he's always sailing off somewhere for another adventure? No, Vaina, I will not be your wife."

Before Vaina could plead his case, Ilmarinen came in. When he pulled off his hat, the firelight gleamed brightly on his thick golden hair. It was over a year since Seppo had lived with them to make the magic Sampo. He seemed now even more attractive than the Maid remembered.

"Did you really bring singing birds from Kalevala on your sledge, Seppo?" asked the Maid.

"Six cuckoos and seven bluebirds," he answered shyly.

The Maid of the North brought the large cup of mead to Ilmarinen and put it into his hands.

But Seppo only held it before him carefully. "I will not drink the mead cup until I have your answer. For many, many months I have thought of you and longed for you. If you do not accept me this time, I will not return again."

The Maid gave him a radiant smile. Before she could speak, Louhi cut in quickly.

"I see she has made her choice. That's all very well, but there's something you must do for me first. Not far away there is a Field of Vipers that must be plowed."

"Yes, yes . . . of course," stammered Ilmarinen.

"Hiisi the Evil One dumped them there, and it's a great nuisance to me—" began Louhi. Then she saw that old Vainamoinen had left quietly to return to his boat. She hurried after him to be sure he was well stocked with provisions.

When the Maid and Seppo were alone, he turned to her with a puzzled frown. "I don't think your mother wants you to marry me. A Field of Vipers! Does she want me killed so you will marry Vaina?"

"I would never marry Vaina," she assured him. "But this task is not as difficult as it sounds, my dear. I can tell you how to do it. Forge for yourself a coat of mail, iron boots, and iron gloves, so the vipers cannot touch you. Then forge a plow of gold and silver to make them leave. With these things you will plow the field safely."

Ilmarinen went off to the forge where he had once made the magic Sampo. He followed the Maid's instructions, then set off, clad in the iron garments.

The Field of Vipers, filled with small, twisting serpents, was a horrible place to see. Seppo hesitated but a moment before setting the gold and silver plow into the field. Chanting the spell against serpents, he strode into the mass of writhing snakes. Their fangs snapped, but could not harm him through his metal garments. In a very short time they all slipped away from the field and disappeared. When the field was plowed in clean, even strips, he returned to the farmhouse.

"I have plowed the field, Mistress," he told Louhi. "Now may I marry your daughter?"

"Not yet," said crafty Louhi. "You must capture the Great Bear and the Great Wolf that live in the forest of Tuoni, the Lord of the Dead. Bring them to me—and then we'll see." Louhi knew very well that many heroes had tried to capture these beasts without success.

Seppo went off to find the Maid. "My love, I think your mother wishes me harm!" he exclaimed. "She wants me to capture the Great Bear and the Great Wolf from the Land of the Dead! I'll be torn to pieces!"

"Perhaps my mother only wants to be sure I marry a great hero," said the Maid thoughtfully. "Do not worry, Seppo. I know how it can be done. Listen carefully. Sit on a rock under the spray of a waterfall and forge two iron muzzles. With these the Great Bear and the Great Wolf of Tuoni can be easily captured."

Ilmarinen followed the Maid's advice. When he had forged the huge muzzles of hard iron and attached chains to them, he set out for the forest of Tuoni. He crept cautiously through the forest until he came upon the Great Bear. Leaping from behind, he muzzled the beast and left him chained to a tree. He captured the Wolf in the same way. Then, using all his strength, he dragged the two animals back to Louhi's farm.

"Here they are," he panted. "Much good may they do you!"

Louhi nodded in approval. "It seems you're a proper hero after all. Now there's just one more task before I arrange the wedding feast. Bring me the Great Pike that swims in Tuoni's river—without using a net or a line." *Plenty of heroes have tried* that, she thought, *and not returned.*

Ilmarinen left her and again sought out the Maid to tell her of the task that had been laid on him. "This is too much!" he cried angrily. "Catch that monstrous Pike with my bare hands? He would chew me up in a moment!"

"My darling, only you can do it," she said proudly. "I will tell you how. Forge a huge bird of fire and flame, with claws of iron. The bird will catch the Pike for you, and you will not be harmed."

Once more, Ilmarinen set to work in the forge. When he had made the huge metal bird of fire and flame, he climbed on its back and was borne swiftly to the shores of the river of Tuonela. There they waited until the Great Pike rose to the surface. And what a monster he proved to be! His body was as long as seven boats, and his sharp teeth filled a mouth as long as two rake handles.

The iron bird leaped onto the Pike at once, seizing it in its claws. A long and furious battle raged between them, for the Pike had great power in its jaws and tried to drag the bird of iron under the water. At last the Great Pike was killed, and the huge bird flew up to the top of a pine tree with the fish. There he ripped it apart with its claws and began to eat it.

With a roar of rage, Seppo ordered the bird to stop. "I must bring that Pike to Louhi!" he shouted. "Drop it at once!"

The great bird tossed down the head. Then, with a sweep of its huge wings, it flew off out of sight with the remainder of the Pike in its beak.

Ilmarinen dragged the long head of the Pike back to Louhi's farm.

"Here's the head of your Great Pike!" he growled. "You can make a long bench from the bones if you wish!"

"I asked for the Great Pike itself, not the head," Louhi began. But when she saw the expression on Seppo's face, she decided to drop the matter.

"You can marry the Maid," she said hastily, "and sorry I'll be to lose her."

And so it was settled at last. While Seppo hurried back to his home with the news, Louhi began the preparations for the wedding feast.

An enormous hall was built to feed and house the guests. The Great Ox of Carelia was slaughtered to provide hundreds of barrels of meat and hundreds of barrels of sausages. Hundreds of barrels of ale and mead were brewed. More than half of all the fish in the rivers and lakes were caught. There seemed no end to the mountains of food and drink.

Never had the North Land seen such a feast! All the people of the North Land and all the people of Kalevala were invited to the wedding, and most of them came. The people flocked to Louhi's farm from all directions—by sledge, by boat, by skis. And Seppo, at the head of a small army of joyful kinfolk, arrived on the appointed day.

The feasting and singing and merrymaking went on for seven days and seven nights. Then at last it was time for the Maid of the North to take off her richly embroidered wedding garments and prepare for the journey south to Kalevala.

Seppo's sledge was ready, gay with singing birds on the reins. The bridal couple were settled under fur robes. The whip cracked and they moved off amid the cheers and good wishes of the guests.

And that is the story of how the Maid of the North left her beloved North Country to live with the Master Smith Ilmarinen in Kalevala.

A Celtic Tale

.   .   .

*T*here once was a young woman who was alone in the world, except for her child. She had only a cow, a few chickens, and a small garden to get along on. To earn a little money she would go out to work in the fields at haying time and harvest time.

One day she laid the baby on a rough piece of cloth in the shade of an old hawthorn tree, picked up a scythe, and took her place with the hay mowers.

The lass had mowed several lengths of the field when she heard the baby wailing with hunger. She hurried to the hawthorn tree, thinking that the wailing did not sound at all like her sweet-tempered baby.

When she got there, she saw that it was not her plump, dark-haired child that lay in the shade—it was a thin, scrawny baby with wisps of fair hair.

She ran up and down the side of the field, searching for her own child, but there was not a sign of him. She called to the other mowers. No one had seen her baby, nor had they seen anyone come to the hawthorn tree.

She went back to the wailing baby, her heart breaking with grief. Then, because she was a kindhearted lass, she took pity on the thin, pale child. She could not bear to see him so hungry, so she nursed him.

With a heavy heart she returned to the mowing, for she needed the money. But when the day was over, she felt she could not abandon the sickly child in the field all night. She carried the small bundle home with her.

That evening and all the next day, she went up and down the lanes of the village, asking everyone she met if they had seen her dark-haired, rosy-cheeked baby.

No one had seen him. "The fairy folk have taken your child and left a sickly one of their own in his place," she was told. "You must get rid of the changeling if you want your own back." But the advice they gave on how to get rid of the changeling was so cruel that she could not follow it.

She made up her mind to get her own child back from the fairies, though how she was to do it she did not know. Nonetheless, as the weeks passed, she fed and cared for the strange, pale child as best she could. He no longer looked quite so frail and thin. His wisps of hair grew into thick red-gold curls; he would soon be as plump and healthy as her own child.

"Your mother should see you now," thought the lass one day. "You're so healthy and handsome she wouldn't know you!"

The summer had gone before the lass heard of an old woman who was said to know the ways of the fairy folk. Although the woman lived alone out on the moors, some distance away, the lass trudged off at once to consult her.

After she had told the old woman of her stolen child, she said, "Do you know where the fairy folk dwell? I'm determined to get my own child back."

"You're a brave lass," said the old woman. "But do you know the danger in it?"

"That doesn't matter," answered the lass.

"They can lame or blind those who annoy them—or do worse mischief," warned the old woman. "They could keep you prisoner under the fairy hill forever."

"I wouldn't like that, but if I were with my own child again—"

"But, lass, if you go to their fairy hill, you'd be putting yourself in their power!" When the lass did not answer, the woman sighed, "Well, if you won't be warned, I'll tell you what I can."

"That is what I came for," said the lass.

"The fairy folk live under that big hill out yonder on the moors," said the woman. "They don't come out very often, and when they do, there are few that can see them."

"Have you seen them?" asked the girl directly.

"Sometimes," the woman admitted. "I did them a favor long ago, and they've been good neighbors to me."

"I want to see the Queen," said the girl firmly. "She will know who took my baby."

"The Queen and all the folk come out of the hill on Halloween to ride abroad. That I do know. But it will do you no good. She'll fly into a rage if you demand your child back."

"I can try," said the girl.

"Don't expect the Queen to take pity on your grief. Fairy folk have no hearts, no hearts at all. 'Tis the way they are made."

"I'll not ask for pity," said the lass. "All I'll ask is a fair exchange."

"It's not a thing I'd dare to do," said the old woman.

The lass walked out to the fairy hill at once, for she thought she might find a way in. She walked all around it, poking at rocks, pulling at bushes, but she could see no opening at all. At last she gave up and came away. She made up her mind she would come back on Halloween.

The weeks passed slowly. Finally the nuts ripened and fell, and the leaves turned yellow and red and drifted from the trees.

On Halloween the lass milked the cow and fed the baby, and wrapping him against the chill wind, she started off for the fairy hill.

The night was dark, with heavy clouds scudding across the moon. It was a long way out to the fairy hill on the moors, and the baby grew heavy in her arms. She paused to rest now and then, but not for long. When she reached the moors, it was so dark she couldn't see the hill. Twice she turned the wrong way.

At last she reached the hill and sank wearily to the ground. She had no way of knowing if she was too early or too late—nor even which part of the hill would open to send the fairy folk forth.

She waited in the silence and the dark. After a little while her head nodded in weariness, and she dozed.

It was near midnight when she was jerked awake by the sound of silvery bells. Flowing out of the hill, some distance from where she sat, was a troop of fairy folk. The Queen rode before them on a white steed. In the glow of their own eerie fairy light, she could see that the Queen was splendidly dressed in green and gold, her gleaming red-gold hair flying behind her.

The lass jumped to her feet, but the fairy folk came out of the hill with the rush of a strong wind and were off in a flurry of jingling bells. The eerie fairy glow died away, and she was left standing on the empty moor in the moonlight.

For a few moments she was overcome with despair. Then she said to herself with a sigh, "I never expected it would be easy!"

She stood for a moment, fixing in her mind by means of rocks and bushes just where the fairy hill had opened. "I'll stand right in their path next time," she thought.

She went back to where the changeling lay asleep and carried him all the long way home. It was near dawn when she opened the door to her small cottage, and there was a day's work ahead of her.

The winter passed, cold with sleet and icy rain. The fair-haired changeling grew sturdier, but he was a silent child with a faraway look in his eyes. One spring day the lass met the old woman at market.

"I see you still have the changeling," said the old woman.

"Yes," said the lass. "My eyes closed for weariness on Halloween, but I shall try again. Will the fairy folk come out on May Eve?"

"They should," said the old woman. Then she added kindly, "Come early to my cottage and rest yourself before you set out."

"Thank you," said the lass. "I'll do that."

On May Eve she arrived at the old woman's cottage early. The changeling was now a plump, handsome child, although his skin still had the whiteness of fairy kind.

As soon as the sun set, the lass and the child went off to the fairy hill. She put the child to sleep beside her and settled down for a long wait.

This time, when the hill opened with the jingling of silver bells on bridles, the lass was ready. The Queen rode out, splendidly radiant, at the head of the fairy folk.

The lass had placed herself in their path. Now she ran forward and caught the bridle of the Queen's steed. The Queen raised her staff as if to strike.

"Who dares to halt the Queen?" she cried in cold anger.

But before the Queen could blind or cripple her, the lass cried out, "If you please, ma'am, I have brought you a gift."

The whole company of folk halted behind the Queen were still.

"A gift? What manner of talk is this?" asked the Queen irritably, but her interest was caught.

At this moment the child woke, cried aloud, and stood up.

"Who is that child? Why do you bring him here?"

The lass went to the child and held him firmly at her side. "He's a handsome child, isn't he?"

"Is this the gift?" asked the Queen coolly, but her eyes stared at the child.

"In a manner of speaking," said the lass, just as coolly. "He was left in a hayfield last summer—a thin, sickly thing. Do you remember?"

The Queen said nothing.

"I took him home with me, fed him, cared for him, brought him to health. I was pleased to do a favor for one of your women. Do you know his mother?"

"I *am* his mother," said the Queen curtly.

"I thought he'd be of royal stock—he's that handsome and clever a child!" said the lass, thinking a bit of flattery would do no harm.

"So you've brought him back to the fairy folk!" said the Queen in surprise. "Didn't you want to keep him?"

"He's of fairy stock; I don't think he'll thrive for long in the outside world," said the lass. "And that seems a pity."

"Hand him up to me," said the Queen. "I want to see if this is really my child."

"No," said the lass. "I've done you a favor, and now I ask one in return. I want my own son back."

The Queen frowned. "I could seize the child."

"You could," admitted the lass, and her heart shook within her. "But I did you a favor, nursed your child, shared the little food I had with him. It's said that fairy folk repay favors honestly. All I ask is a fair exchange. I want my own child back."

The Queen laughed. "You have cool courage, girl. Don't you

know I could seize both of you and keep you in our hill?"

"I know that," said the lass steadily. "But I was thinking you'd want to repay the favor. He's a fine, handsome prince for your court."

Abruptly the Queen called to the folk behind her, "Bring the dark-haired child." Then, to the lass, "Now let me have this one."

"No," said the lass. "Not until I have my own in my arms."

"A stubborn lass!" commented the Queen. "You have no fear at all; I admire that. Well, here he is."

When the lass had her own child on the grass beside her, she handed the fair-haired boy up to the Queen.

The Queen held the child before her on the saddle. She said coolly, "He *is* a healthy, handsome child. You took care of him well." Then, looking down at the lass holding her own child tightly in her arms, she added, "Go in peace. The favor and goodwill of the fairy folk will stay with your child all his life."

With a rush of wind and a jingle of bells, they were away. The eerie fairy glow was gone. The lass was alone on the dark, empty moor.

Carrying her own child, she walked with a light heart to the old woman's cottage.

As the Queen had promised, good fortune and prosperity came to the lass and her child and stayed with them ever after.

GAWAIN AND THE LADY RAGNELL

An English Tale

• • •

Long ago, in the days of King Arthur, the finest knight in all Britain was the king's nephew Gawain. He was, by reputation, the bravest in battle, the wisest, the most courteous, the most compassionate, and the most loyal to his king.

One day in late summer, Gawain was with Arthur and the knights of the court at Carlisle in the north. The King returned from the day's hunting looking so pale and shaken that Gawain followed him at once to his chamber.

"What has happened, my lord?" asked Gawain with concern.

Arthur sat down heavily. "I had a very strange encounter in Inglewood forest . . . I hardly know what to make of it." And he related to Gawain what had occurred.

"Today I hunted a great white stag," said Arthur. "The stag at

3 5

last escaped me and I was alone, some distance from my men. Suddenly a tall, powerful man appeared before me with sword upraised."

"And you were unarmed!"

"Yes. I had only my bow and a dagger in my belt. He threatened to kill me," Arthur went on. "And he swung his sword as though he meant to cut me down on the spot! Then he laughed horribly and said he would give me one chance to save my life."

"Who was this man?" cried Gawain. "Why should he want to kill you?"

"He said his name was Sir Gromer, and he sought revenge for the loss of his northern lands."

"A chieftain from the north!" exclaimed Gawain. "But what is this one chance he spoke of?"

"I gave him my word I would meet him one year from to-day, unarmed, at the same spot, with the answer to a question!" said Arthur.

Gawain started to laugh, but stopped at once when he saw Arthur's face. "A question! Is it a riddle? And one year to find the answer? That should not be hard!"

"If I can bring him the true answer to the question, 'What is it that women most desire, above all else?' my life will be spared." Arthur scowled. "He is sure I will fail. It must be a foolish riddle that no one can answer."

"My lord, we have one year to search the kingdom for answers," said Gawain confidently. "I will help you. Surely one of the answers will be the right one."

"No doubt you are right—someone will know the answer." Arthur looked more cheerful. "The man is mad, but a chieftain will keep his word."

For the next twelve months, Arthur and Gawain asked the question from one corner of the kingdom to the other. Then at last the appointed day drew near. Although they had many answers, Arthur was worried.

"With so many answers to choose from, how do we know which is the right one?" he asked in despair. "Not one of them has the ring of truth."

A few days before he was to meet Sir Gromer, Arthur rode out alone through the golden gorse and purple heather. The track led upward toward a grove of great oaks. Arthur, deep in thought, did not look up until he reached the edge of the oak wood. When he raised his head, he pulled up suddenly in astonishment.

Before him was a grotesque woman. She was almost as wide as she was high, her skin was mottled green, and spikes of weedlike hair covered her head. Her face seemed more animal than human.

The woman's eyes met Arthur's fearlessly. "You are Arthur the king," she said in a harsh, croaking voice. "In two days time you must meet Sir Gromer with the answer to a question."

Arthur turned cold with fear. He stammered, "Yes . . . yes . . . that is true. Who are you? How did you know of this?"

"I am the lady Ragnell. Sir Gromer is my stepbrother. You haven't found the true answer, have you?"

"I have many answers," Arthur replied curtly. "I do not see how my business concerns you." He gathered up the reins, eager to be gone.

"You do not have the right answer." Her certainty filled him with a sense of doom. The harsh voice went on, "But I know the answer to Sir Gromer's question."

Arthur turned back in hope and disbelief. "You do? Tell me the true answer to his question, and I will give you a large bag of gold."

"I have no use for gold," she said coldly.

"Nonsense, my good woman. With gold you can buy anything you want!" He hesitated a moment, for the huge, grotesque face with the cool, steady eyes unnerved him. He went on hurriedly,

"What is it you want? Jewelry? Land? Whatever you want I will pay you—that is, if you truly have the right answer."

"I know the answer. I promise you that!" She paused. "What I demand in return is that the knight Gawain become my husband."

There was a moment of shocked silence. Then Arthur cried, "Impossible! You ask the impossible, woman!"

She shrugged and turned to leave.

"Wait, wait a moment!" Rage and panic overwhelmed him, but he tried to speak reasonably.

"I offer you gold, land, jewels. I cannot give you my nephew. He is his own man. He is not mine to give!"

"I did not ask you to *give* me the knight Gawain," she rebuked him. "If Gawain himself agrees to marry me, I will give you the answer. Those are my terms."

"Impossible!" he sputtered. "I could not bring him such a proposal."

"If you should change your mind, I will be here tomorrow," said she, and disappeared into the oak woods.

Shaken from the weird encounter, Arthur rode homeward at a slow pace.

"Save my own life at Gawain's expense? Never!" he thought. "Loathsome woman! I could not even speak of it to Gawain."

But the afternoon air was soft and sweet with birdsong, and the fateful meeting with Sir Gromer weighed on him heavily. He was torn by the terrible choice facing him.

Gawain rode out from the castle to meet the king. Seeing Arthur's pale, strained face, he exclaimed, "My lord! Are you ill? What has happened?"

"Nothing . . . nothing at all." But he could not keep silent long. "The colossal impudence of the woman! A monster, that's what she is! That creature, daring to give me terms!"

"Calm yourself, uncle," Gawain said patiently. "What woman? Terms for what?"

Arthur sighed. "She knows the answer to the question. I didn't intend to tell you."

"Why not? Surely that's good news! What is the answer?"

"She will not tell me until her terms are met," said the king heavily. "But I assure you, I refuse to consider her proposal!"

Gawain smiled. "You talk in riddles yourself, uncle. Who is this woman who claims to know the answer? What is her proposal?"

Seeing Gawain's smiling, expectant face, Arthur at first could not speak. Then, with his eyes averted, the king told Gawain the whole story, leaving out no detail.

"The lady Ragnell is Sir Gromer's stepsister? Yes, I think she would know the right answer," Gawain said thoughtfully. "How fortunate that I will be able to save your life!"

"No! I will not let you sacrifice yourself!" Arthur cried.

"It is my choice and my decision," Gawain answered. "I will return with you tomorrow and agree to the marriage—on condition that the answer she supplies is the right one to save your life."

Early the following day, Gawain rode out with Arthur. But not even meeting the loathsome lady face to face could shake his resolve. Her proposal was accepted.

Gawain bowed courteously. "If on the morrow your answer saves the king's life, we will be wed."

On the fateful morning, Gawain watched the king stow a parchment in his saddlebag. "I'll try all these answers first," said Arthur.

They rode together for the first part of the journey. Then Arthur, unarmed as agreed, rode on alone to Inglewood to meet Sir Gromer.

The tall, powerful chieftain was waiting, his broadsword glinting in the sun.

Arthur read off one answer, then another, and another. Sir Gromer shook his head in satisfaction.

"No, you have not the right answer!" he said raising his sword high. "You've failed, and now—"

"Wait!" Arthur cried. "I have one more answer. What a woman desires above all else is the power of sovereignty—the right to exercise her own will."

With a loud oath the man dropped his sword. "You did not find that answer by yourself!" he shouted. "My cursed stepsister, Ragnell, gave it to you. Bold, interfering hussy! I'll run her through with my sword . . . I'll lop off her head . . ." Turning, he plunged into the forest, a string of horrible curses echoing behind him.

Arthur rode back to where Gawain waited with the monstrous Ragnell. They returned to the castle in silence. Only the grotesque Lady Ragnell seemed in good spirits.

The news spread quickly throughout the castle. Gawain, the finest knight in the land, was to marry this monstrous creature! Some tittered and laughed at the spectacle; others said the lady Ragnell must possess very great lands and estates; but mostly there was stunned silence.

Arthur took his nephew aside nervously. "Must you go through with it at once? A postponement perhaps?"

Gawain looked at him steadily. "I gave my promise, my lord. The lady Ragnell's answer saved your life. Would you have me—"

"Your loyalty makes me ashamed! Of course you cannot break your word." And Arthur turned away.

The marriage took place in the abbey. Afterward, with Gawain and the lady Ragnell sitting at the high dais table beside the king and queen, the strange wedding feast began.

"She takes the space of two women on the chair," muttered the knight Gareth. "Poor Gawain!"

"I would not marry such a creature for all the land in Christendom!" answered his companion.

An uneasy silence settled on the hall. Only the monstrous Lady Ragnell displayed good spirits and good appetite. Throughout the long day and evening, Gawain remained pleasant and courteous. In no way did his manner toward his strange bride show other than kind attention.

The wedding feast drew to a close. Gawain and his bride were conducted to their chamber and were at last alone.

The lady Ragnell gazed at her husband thoughtfully.

"You have kept your promise well and faithfully," she observed.

Gawain inclined his head. "I could not do less, my lady."

"You've shown neither revulsion nor pity," she said. After a pause she went on, "Come now, we are wedded! I am waiting to be kissed."

Gawain went to her at once and kissed her. When he stepped back, there stood before him a slender young woman with gray eyes and a serene, smiling face.

His scalp tingled in shock. "What manner of sorcery is this?" he cried hoarsely.

"Do you prefer me in this form?" she smiled and turned slowly in a full circle.

But Gawain backed away warily. "I . . . yes . . . of course . . . but . . . I don't understand . . ." For this sudden evidence of sorcery, with its unknown powers, made him confused and uneasy.

"My stepbrother, Sir Gromer, had always hated me," said the lady Ragnell. "Unfortunately, through his mother, he has a knowledge of sorcery, and so he changed me into a monstrous creature. He said I must live in that shape until I could persuade the greatest knight in Britain to willingly choose me for his bride. He said it would be an impossible condition to meet!"

"Why did he hate you so cruelly?"

Her lips curled in amusement. "He thought me bold and un-womanly because I defied him. I refused his commands both for my property and my person."

Gawain said with admiration, "You won the 'impossible' condition he set, and now his evil spell is broken!"

"Only in part." Her clear gray eyes held his. "You have a choice, my dear Gawain, which way I will be. Would you have me in this, my own shape, at night and my former ugly shape by day? Or would you have me grotesque at night in our chamber, and my own shape in the castle by day? Think carefully before you choose."

Gawain was silent only a moment. He knelt before her and touched her hand.

"It is a choice I cannot make, my dear Ragnell. It concerns you. Whatever you choose to be—fair by day or fair by night—I will willingly abide by it."

Ragnell released a long, deep breath. The radiance in her face overwhelmed him.

"You have answered well, dearest Gawain, for your answer has broken Gromer's evil spell completely. The last condition he set has been met! For he said that if, after marriage to the greatest knight in Britain, my husband freely gave me the power of choice, the power to exercise my own free will, the wicked enchantment would be broken forever."

Thus, in wonder and in joy, began the marriage of Gawain and the lady Ragnell.

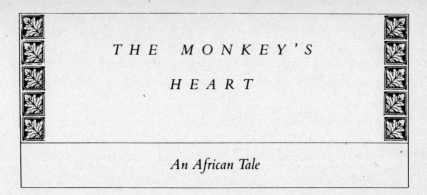

THE MONKEY'S
HEART

An African Tale

. . .

*T*here once was a small gray monkey who came every day at sunrise to a large tree that grew near the sea. This tree grew so close to the edge of the sea that some of its branches hung out over the water. The tree bore a sweet red fruit, and the monkey swung herself from branch to branch, eating her fill.

One day as the monkey sat eating the red berries, she saw a shark swimming in the sea below her. The shark was watching the monkey with greedy eyes.

"Hello, friend," called the monkey. "Would you like a berry?"

"I was hoping you would ask," said the shark. "I would love to have some berries. I'm very tired of eating fish. They taste so salty."

"I don't care much for salty food myself," said the monkey. She pulled off a berry and threw it down to the shark.

The first red berry hit the shark on the nose. So the shark rolled over on his back and opened his big jaws. It was quite easy then to throw the berries right into his mouth.

"Thank you! Thank you!" cried the shark. "I never ate anything that tasted so good! Would you throw down more?"

The monkey did so. And every morning after that, the shark waited underneath the tree. The monkey picked the red berries and shared them with the shark.

"You are so kind and generous," said the shark one day. "I wish I could do something for you."

"I can't think of anything," said the monkey. "I'm not fond of fish."

The shark began to tell the monkey of the wonders of the sea, of all the strange creatures who lived there. He told her of strange, faraway lands one could visit. "I could show you many new, interesting things if you'd come with me," said the shark.

The monkey was not at all sure she wanted to travel. "I would get all wet," she said, "and I do hate the water."

"You wouldn't get wet at all," cried the shark. "You could ride on my back quite safely. I will take you to visit the king of my country."

"In that case," said the monkey, "I'd be very glad to go with you."

The monkey dropped down from the tree and landed neatly on the shark's back. True to his word, the shark swam off carefully, and the monkey didn't get a bit wet.

The monkey was delighted with the ride. After they had traveled a few hours, the shark said, "Oh, I forgot to tell you! The king of my country is very ill. The only thing that will cure him is a monkey's heart."

The monkey sat very still. Then she said lightly, "That *is* too bad. I'm sorry for your king, but you should have told me this before we started out."

"It's a small matter," said the shark. "I just forgot about it."

"You see, I have no heart with me," said the monkey. "I left it behind."

"What do you mean, you have no heart?" cried the shark.

"Monkeys always leave their hearts at home when they travel," said she. "Before we set off, I took mine out and hung it on a branch of the berry tree."

"What a silly thing to do!" said the shark crossly. "You should not travel without your heart. I'll take you back at once so you can get it."

"It does seem like a lot of trouble for you," said the monkey. "But perhaps you're right; we had better go back for it."

"No trouble at all!" said the shark. Turning around, he swam back so fast they were back at the tree in an hour.

At once the monkey caught a low-hanging branch and swung up into the tree. In a moment she was high and safe among the leaves. Curling herself up, she happily went to sleep.

The shark swam round and round under the tree as he waited. At last he called out loudly, "Where are you?"

The monkey woke up and saw that the shark was still there.

"I'm up here taking a nap," she called back.

"Have you got your heart? It's time we were going."

"Going where?" asked the monkey.

"We're going to my country with your heart. Have you forgotten?"

The monkey laughed. "You must be crazy! Do you take me for a silly donkey?"

"Don't talk nonsense," said the shark. "Come down at once,

or we may be too late to save the king's life."

"I'm not coming down to travel with you," said the monkey. "Only a silly donkey would do *that* twice!"

The shark thought about that for a moment. Then he said, "Perhaps a donkey's heart will do." (For he was not sure what a donkey was.) "Where will I find a silly donkey?"

"I can't tell you that," said the monkey, "but I can tell you what happened to the washerman's silly donkey."

And this is the story she told:

•   •   •

A washerman lived in a small house close to a great forest. With him lived a donkey who carried the man's baskets back and forth to the village nearby. The donkey finally grew bored with this life, so he ran away deep into the woods. There he lived very well on grass and nuts. With nothing to do all day, he grew fatter and fatter.

One day a hare passing by saw the fat donkey sleeping on a bed of leaves. Farther on, she passed a lion's den. The lion was quite weak and thin, for she had been sick.

The hare stopped a safe distance away. "How are you feeling today?" asked the hare politely.

"Much better," answered the lion. "But I am still too weak to get up and hunt."

"There is a nice fat donkey not far from here," said the hare.

"Why tell me that?" said the lion crossly. "You know I'm too weak to go after it. And I am very hungry!"

"Perhaps I could bring the donkey to you," said the hare.

"If you could do that," said the lion in surprise, "I would be your friend for life!"

The hare hopped back to the donkey.

"Good morning," said the hare. "I have some very good news for you."

"Really?" said the donkey. "How kind you are! What is this news?"

"My friend the lion has heard how handsome and clever and charming you are. She is quite in love with you and would like you to come visit her."

The donkey wiggled his ears in pleasure. "Where is this lovely lion?"

"She has been very ill; she is still too weak to walk. But I can take you to her."

The donkey stood up and shook the leaves from his coat. "Yes, of course I will come. Such an honor! I suppose that if we marry, I shall be king of the beasts?"

The hare didn't answer. She laughed to herself as she ran on ahead to lead the donkey to the lion's den. When they arrived, the lion was sitting up, looking pale and thin.

"I'm so glad to see you," said the lion. "Please come in."

The hare said she had other things to do, and hurried away. But the donkey went into the lion's den.

"Ahem," said the donkey, swishing his tail. "Hare told me you have fallen in love with—" He stopped short in surprise and terror. The lion was crouched in the corner and her eyes were blazing. With a loud roar she leaped at the donkey.

The donkey jumped to one side just in time. He gave her a sharp kick in the ribs. The lion rolled over, clawing the donkey; the donkey bit the lion on the shoulder. Then the lion sprang at him with open jaws, but the donkey rolled over, and with another sharp kick, he knocked the lion across the den. Scrambling to his feet, he ran off into the forest.

Two or three weeks passed. The donkey's scars healed, and the lion was now strong and well.

One day the little hare stopped a safe distance from the cave and called out, "I see you are quite well again."

"Yes, indeed," said the lion. "But you promised me a donkey for my dinner, and all I got was bites and kicks. If I could get hold of that donkey, I'd tear him to pieces!"

"Yes, yes, I did promise you a donkey," said the hare. "Shall I try to bring him back here to you?"

"Do that, and I will be your friend for life," said the lion.

The hare hurried off. This time the donkey was quite far away; but the hare found him at last, rolling in moss to scratch his back.

"Good morning," said the hare. "I see your coat is as handsome as ever! The lion sent me to find you. She would like you to come see her again."

"Again!" cried the donkey as he stood up. "I don't know if I will. Last time she scratched me badly. I was very frightened."

"She was only trying to kiss you," said the hare. "But you kicked her and bit her. That made her angry."

"Oh, I see," said the silly donkey. "Are you sure?"

"Lions are like that," said the hare. "Come along and at least talk to her."

So the silly donkey once more followed the hare through the forest. This time the lion sat hidden behind a tree. When the donkey passed, she leaped out and, with a blow of her paw, knocked him dead.

.   .   .

"Is that the end of the story?" asked the shark.

"That's the end," said the monkey.

And the shark swam away, saying to himself, "I wish I had found a silly donkey instead of a clever monkey!"

THE TWELVE
HUNTSMEN

A German Tale

• • •

$\mathcal{A}$ long time ago, in the forests of the Rhineland, there lived a wealthy nobleman with his daughter, Katrine. He had no son. Katrine was his only child, and from an early age she had ridden out to hunt with her father. He had taught her not simply to shoot an arrow straight and true, but all the skills of hunting. When the lady Katrine reached the usual age for marriage, many suitors came to her father's castle. However, Katrine was well content with her life. She said she had no interest in marriage, and the suitors were refused.

Then one day a young prince, Wilhelm, traveling leisurely through the country, came to stay at the nobleman's castle. As his visit lengthened from weeks into months, Katrine and the young prince fell in love. The betrothal followed, and the prince gave Katrine his ring.

Not long after this, a messenger arrived seeking the prince. Wilhelm's father, the king, was very ill and requested his son to come to him at once. The young man bade farewell to Katrine, promising to return as soon as he could.

When the young prince arrived at his distant kingdom, he found his father close to death. On his deathbed, the king demanded his son's promise to marry a princess of a neighboring kingdom, for this union of the two kingdoms had long been the king's wish. He had already arranged the match with the father of the princess.

Wilhelm tried to tell his father he had made another choice. But so great was his grief at his father's suffering that he at last promised to do as his father wished. Very soon after this the father died, and the young prince became king.

Now, on the grounds of the castle the old king had kept a lion much noted for his wisdom. One day the lion said to the grieving Wilhelm, "Do not be in a hurry to marry the princess. Postpone the marriage until the end of the year's mourning period." This suited the new king very well, and he took the lion's advice.

Although the lady Katrine looked forward eagerly to the prince's return, she waited quite patiently for some time. There were the maids of honor to select, and plans to be made for a splendid wedding. But when months passed with no word from Wilhelm, she became hurt and then angry.

"He has forgotten me so quickly!" she exclaimed bitterly to her father. "He was not worth my love!"

Wishing to reassure his daughter, her father said, "The prince Wilhelm may have had an accident or fallen ill."

This possibility made her so silent with grief that her father said, "Have patience, my dear. If we hear nothing at the end of a year, I will send a messenger to his father's kingdom. Now tell me what you would like to make you happy, and I will give it to you."

"I can no longer be merry or patient, father. I wish to know the truth. If the prince no longer loves me, I will forget him. But if he lies ill, I must go to him."

For a few days she considered how she could best learn the truth of the matter. The plan she formed was simple. The eleven maids of honor she had chosen were her friends and companions. Like herself, they were young and very capable horsewomen.

"I will take my eleven companions to the prince's kingdom in disguise as huntsmen," she told her father. "In that way I can learn for myself whether my betrothed is false or true."

While the green hunting clothes were cut and sewn, the twelve maidens practiced the duties of huntsmen under the chief forester. At last the day came when the twelve companions, their long hair cut short, left the castle dressed as huntsmen. They rode through the forest and mountain passes to the distant kingdom of the prince.

As soon as they arrived in the kingdom, Katrine learned from a shepherd that the prince Wilhelm was now king and in good health, although sad and quiet since the death of his father. Katrine rode grimly on with her eleven huntsmen until they arrived at the king's castle.

Katrine's request for an audience with the king was granted. Standing proudly in the king's chamber with her eleven huntsmen, she asked that the king take them into his service. The trim, handsome appearance of the twelve green-clad youths captured the king's interest. He did not recognize the lady Katrine at all, but he agreed to employ the twelve huntsmen.

They had not been in service at the castle very long before they heard talk that the king was expected to marry a princess from a nearby kingdom when the mourning period was ended.

Katrine's first thought was to return at once to her own country. She said to her companions, "So this is the truth of the matter! He has forgotten our betrothal and plans to wed another!"

"Let us stay longer," they counseled. "It is said the king is bound by a promise to his dying father. Do not believe the worst of Wilhelm until you are sure he does indeed prefer another to you."

Katrine agreed to this, and the twelve huntsmen continued in the king's service.

One day the old lion said to the king, "Your twelve huntsmen are not men. They are women."

"That is absurd!" said the king. "Of course they are men!"

"Test them and see. Spread peas on the floor where they will walk. Women walk lightly and will scatter the peas. Men tread firmly and will crush them."

The king followed the lion's advice. He had peas scattered on the floor of his chamber before he summoned the huntsmen. But Katrine and her maidens had trained themselves to walk as men. They trod firmly on the peas, crushing them beneath their boots.

"You are wrong," said the king to the lion. "I tested them and they are men."

"I know they are women," said the lion. "Have spinning wheels brought to the hall or antechamber they must pass through. Women always look at spinning wheels with eager interest. Men never notice them."

The spinning wheels were set up in the king's antechamber. But when the huntsmen were again summoned, they walked past and not one glanced at the spinning wheels.

"It is clear you are wrong," said the king to the lion. "The huntsmen showed no interest at all in the spinning wheels." He decided the lion was old and foolish.

"One more test, with bows," said the lion. "Women cannot shoot an arrow as men can."

"They handle their bows as well as any huntsmen," said the king crossly. "I'll have no more of your foolish advice."

The lion turned away sulkily and lay down.

Shortly after this, a messenger came to the king with word that

the princess in the nearby kingdom was growing impatient with the delay. She would arrive within a few weeks, accompanied by her father and attendants, to celebrate her betrothal to the king.

Katrine noticed that the king expressed no pleasure over this news. His face was sad with grief. When Katrine saw him pacing in the garden, sighing with despair, her heart softened.

Then the king left the garden abruptly, called for his horse, and rode recklessly away at a gallop. Katrine saddled her horse and followed him.

After riding some distance into the forest, she came upon the king's horse, which was riderless. Cold with fear, she rode on carefully, searching this way and that until she came upon the king, lying injured by his fall.

"Thank God you've found me, huntsman!" he called. "My leg is broken, and I thought I would lie alone here tonight to be eaten by wolves."

Katrine dismounted and hurried to him. "I followed you, sire, when I saw you ride out alone."

"I am grateful, huntsman. I promise that your devotion and loyalty will be well rewarded!"

"Promise, sire? Do kings keep promises?"

The king stared at his huntsman in surprise. "A king's word is always kept!" he exclaimed. "Were it not for my promise to my father, I would not be in such despair now!"

Katrine pulled off her gloves to care for his injury. "Does a king break one promise to keep another?"

But the king did not answer. He was staring at the ring on the huntsman's finger. "Where did you get that ring? Did the lady Katrine send you?"

"The ring was given to me with the promise of a prince," said Katrine.

At this, the king looked into her eyes and knew her. But his great joy at this discovery gave way almost at once to despair.

"How can I break my promise to my father, given when he lay on his deathbed? I have delayed as long as I could, but the princess grows impatient."

"Such a promise cannot be binding when you were already be-trothed to me!" said Katrine. "Since your father valued the lion's wisdom, why don't you ask him for advice?"

The king agreed to this. "The old fellow is not so foolish after all—for he was right about you and your huntsmen!"

After the king, his injured leg bound with branches, was carried back to the castle on a litter, he had the lion brought to him. When the lion said that the king's betrothal to Katrine released him from the promise he had given his father, the king's last scruple was dissolved.

The king's ministers were sent to explain the situation to the princess, and very soon afterwards the wedding of the king and the lady Katrine was celebrated with great joy and feasting throughout the kingdom.

THE OLD WOMAN
AND THE
RICE CAKES

A Japanese Tale

• • •

Long ago, in Japan, there was a cheerful old woman who lived alone in a small house halfway up a steep hill. She had a few chickens and a pig, but very little else. Quite often she had only one meal a day.

One evening she had just finished making a small bowl of round rice cakes for her dinner, when the bowl slipped and the rice cakes fell to the floor. To her dismay, they rolled right out the doorway. The old woman ran after them.

Once outside, the rice cakes rolled down the steep hill, bouncing over rocks, going faster and faster. The woman scurried down the hill behind them, but she could not catch up with them until they came to rest at the very bottom, near a large slab of rock.

Just as the woman bent over to pick up her rice cakes, a long, blue, scaly arm with a three-fingered, clawlike hand reached out from behind the rock and snatched them from her.

"That's my dinner!" she cried. She peered behind the rock slab, and seeing a small opening, in she went right after her rice cakes.

She found herself in a narrow tunnel. Ahead of her was a large, shambling creature hurrying away.

"Sir!" she called loudly, trotting after him. "My dinner! You've taken my dinner!" But the creature went right on, with the woman close behind him, until they reached a large cave.

The old woman stopped short in surprise. In the cave were several more large creatures. They had horns on their heads, wide mouths that stretched from ear to ear, and three red, staring eyes. She realized she was in a den of Oni, ogres who lived under the ground and came forth only at night. The Japanese Oni, like trolls and demons in other parts of the world, are always bent on evil mischief.

She was, however, more angry than frightened, for the Oni had greedily shared her rice cakes among themselves and gulped them down.

"You're no better than thieves!" she cried. "You've eaten my rice cakes and now I have no dinner!"

But they only sat licking their large, clawlike hands, staring at her so hungrily that she wondered if they were going to eat her next.

Then one of them said, "Did you make the rice cakes?"

"Yes, I did," retorted the old woman. "I make very tasty rice cakes, if I do say so myself."

"Come along, then, and make more!" said he, and he clumped away through a maze of tunnels and caves. The old woman followed him, for she was by now quite hungry and she thought it only fair that the ogres should give her dinner.

But by the time they arrived at the cave full of huge round

cooking pots, she realized she was hopelessly lost. She doubted she could ever find the small hole in the rock where she came in.

The Oni dropped a few grains of rice into a large pot of water.

"That will never make enough rice cakes!" she said crossly.

"Of course it will, stupid creature," he scowled. He picked up a flat wooden stirrer. "Put this into the pot and start stirring."

The woman did as she was told. At once the few grains of rice increased until almost the whole pot was filled. So the old woman made the ogres a huge pile of rice cakes—taking care to eat some herself first, before handing them over.

"I'll be going home now," she announced firmly, "if you'll show me the way back to the entrance."

"Oh, no," growled the Oni. "You will stay here and cook for us."

This did not suit the little old woman at all, but as she looked at the large monsters crowded about, licking their claws, she thought she had better not say so.

Nevertheless, while the woman worked to make piles of rice cakes for the hungry Oni, she thought and thought about how to escape. She soon discovered that the source of the water for cooking the rice was a stream nearby, flowing along between the rock caverns. She thought this must be the same stream that flowed out of the bottom of the hill below her home. Farther on, it became a river, and the people of the village fished from its banks.

But there was no boat to be seen.

"The Oni would not have a boat," thought the old woman. "It's well known the wicked creatures cannot go over water!"

Without a boat, how could she escape? She thought of this as she cooked and stirred—until she saw that one of the large round pots might do very well. They were as big as she was.

The Oni, being night creatures, slept during the day, sprawled in the many caves under the hill. The next day, as soon as they were all asleep, she put the magic stirring paddle in a huge pot and dragged the pot down to the stream.

It floated very nicely, so she hopped in and started to paddle. But the grating sound of the pot being dragged to the stream had wakened a number of Oni nearby. Suddenly they appeared on the side of the stream, shouting in rage.

The old woman paddled faster and faster. Ahead she could see a patch of sunlight where the stream made its way out into the world.

But the stream began to shrink, and grew smaller and smaller. Then she saw that the Oni were drinking up the water, swelling up like monstrous balloons as they sucked in the stream. Rocks and stones began to show in the bed of the stream. The huge pot ground to a halt. All around her, stranded fish flopped about helplessly on the stones.

It seemed the ogres could soon walk across the gravel to seize her. Quick as a wink, the old woman picked up the fish and tossed them, one after another, to the ogres on the banks.

"Have some fish stew!" she called.

The Oni caught the fish in their claws—and because they were always hungry, they opened their wide mouths to gulp down the fish. As soon as they did this, the water rushed out of their mouths again, back into the stream—which, of course, was just what the old woman had hoped would happen.

The round pot floated free, and off the old woman paddled, out of the hill and into broad daylight.

When she had floated down the stream to a safe distance, she paddled over to the nearest bank. Hopping ashore, she pushed the big pot back into the water to drift farther downstream. This, she thought, would mislead the Oni if they should come looking for her. But she kept the magic stirrer with her and climbed safely back up the hill to her house.

The old woman never went hungry again, for with the magic stirrer she was able to make as many rice cakes as she could eat—and she had enough left over to share with her neighbors.

But if any rice cakes fell to the floor and rolled away down the hill, she never went after them.

"Let the Oni have them," she'd say cheerfully. And so, with her chickens, her pig, and plenty of rice for her dinner, she lived very happily the rest of her days.

THE TIGER AND
THE JACKAL

A Punjab Tale from West Pakistan

· · ·

*T*here once was a farmer who went out with his oxen one morning to plow his field.

He had just finished plowing one row when a tiger walked up to him and said, "Good morning, friend. How are you today?"

"Good morning, sir. I am very well, sir," said the farmer. He was shaking with fear, but he felt it wise to be polite.

"I see you have two fine oxen," said the tiger. "I am very hungry. Take off their yokes at once, please, for I intend to eat them."

The farmer's courage returned now that he realized the tiger did not plan to eat *him*. Still, he did not want to give up his oxen for the tiger's meal.

"My friend," said the farmer, "I need these oxen to plow

my field. Surely a brave tiger like you can hunt for a good meal elsewhere!"

"Never mind that!" said the tiger crossly. "Unyoke the oxen. I will be ready to eat them in a moment." And the tiger began to sharpen his teeth and claws on a stone.

"The oxen are very tough and will be hard to eat," pleaded the farmer. "My wife has a fat young milk cow at home. Spare my oxen and I'll bring you the cow."

The tiger agreed to this. He thought a tender young cow would make a much easier meal for him than tough oxen. So he said, "Very well. I will wait here in the field while you go home and get the cow. But bring the cow back as quickly as you can. I'm very hungry."

The farmer took the oxen and went sadly homeward.

"Why do you come home so early in the day?" called his wife. "It is not time for dinner!"

"A tiger came into the field and wanted to eat the oxen," said the farmer. "But I told him he could have the cow instead. Now I must bring him the cow."

"What!" she cried. "You would save your old oxen and give him my beautiful cow? Where will our children get milk? And how can I cook our food without butter?"

"We'll have no food at all unless I plow the field for my crops," said the farmer crossly. "Now untie the cow for me."

"No, I will not give up my cow to the tiger!" said his wife. "Surely you can think of a better way to get rid of the tiger!"

"No, I cannot. He is sitting in my field waiting for me, and he's very hungry."

His wife thought a moment. Then she said, "Go back to the tiger and tell him your wife is bringing the cow. Leave the rest to me."

The farmer did not like to go back to the tiger without the cow. But he had no better idea, so he walked slowly back to the field.

"Where is the cow?" roared the tiger angrily.

"My wife will bring the cow very soon," said the farmer.

At this, the tiger began to prowl about, growling and lashing his tail. The poor farmer's knees shook in terror.

In the meantime, his wife dressed herself in her husband's best clothes. She tied the turban very high on her head to make her look very tall. She took a long knife from the kitchen and put it into her belt. Then she put a saddle on their pony and rode off to the field.

As she drew near, she called out to her husband in a loud voice, "My good man, are there any tigers about? I've been hunting tiger for two days, and I'm hungry for tiger meat!" And she slashed the air above her head with the knife in a very threatening way.

The farmer was so surprised he could not answer.

"Aha!" cried his wife. "Is that a tiger I see hiding in the grass? I ate three tigers for breakfast the other day, and now I'm hungry for more!" And she started to ride toward the tiger.

These words frightened the tiger. He turned tail and bolted into the forest. He ran so fast he knocked over a jackal who was sitting and waiting to feast on the ox bones when the tiger had finished his meal.

"Why are you running away?" called the jackal.

"Run! Run for your life!" cried the tiger. "There is a terribly fierce horseman back in the field! He thinks nothing of eating three tigers for breakfast."

"That was no horseman," laughed the jackal. "That was only the farmer's wife dressed up as a hunter."

The tiger came back slowly. "Are you sure?"

"Did the sun get in your eyes? Didn't you see her hair hanging down from the turban?" asked the jackal impatiently.

The tiger was still doubtful. "He looked like a hunter, and he swung that big knife as if he were going to kill me!"

"Don't give up your meal so easily," cried the brave jackal. "Go back to the field. I will follow and wait in the grass."

The tiger did not like that idea at all. "I think you want me to be killed!"

"No, of course not," said the jackal. He was hungry and impatient. "If you like, we will go together, side by side."

The tiger was still suspicious of the jackal's motives. "You may run away and leave me after we get there."

"We can tie our tails together," said the jackal. "Then I can't run away."

The tiger thought this a good idea. So they tied their tails together in a strong knot, and set off together for the field.

The farmer and his wife were still in the field, laughing over the trick she had played on the tiger. Suddenly they saw the tiger and the jackal trotting toward them with their tails tied together.

The farmer shouted to his wife, "Now the tiger has a jackal with him. Come away! Hurry!"

The wife said no, she would not. She waited until the tiger and jackal were near. Then she called out, "Dear Mr. Jackal, how very kind of you to bring me such a nice fat tiger to eat. After I eat my fill, you can have the bones."

When the tiger heard this, he became wild with terror. He forgot the jackal, and he forgot the knot in their tails. He leaped for the tall grass. Then off he ran, dragging the jackal behind him over stones and through thorn bushes.

The jackal howled and cried for the tiger to stop. But the howls behind him only scared the tiger more, and he ran on until they both collapsed in a heap, more dead than alive.

As for the farmer, he was very proud of his wife's clever trick— for the tiger never came back to their field again.

EAST OF THE SUN, WEST OF THE MOON

A Norwegian Tale

. . .

*O*nce upon a time there were a poor woodcutter and his wife living in the forest, who had so many children that they could scarcely feed and clothe them. They were all fine children, but the bravest and most cheerful was the eldest daughter.

One evening late in the year, when the cold wind blew hard against their little cottage, they heard a loud knock on the door. The father got up from the hearth and went outside to see who it was. A large White Bear stood outside the door, waiting for him.

"Good evening to you," said the White Bear.

"Good evening," said the woodcutter politely.

"I've taken a fancy to your eldest daughter," said the White Bear. "If she will come away to live with me, I can promise your family prosperity and good fortune."

"No, indeed!" said the woodcutter. "I'd rather stay as poor as we are than let my daughter go off to live with a White Bear."

The Bear looked at him sadly. "Perhaps you will change your mind. I'll return next week."

But the woodcutter shook his head and closed the door.

The eldest daughter, who had been standing near the open door, had heard the Bear's words. She thought the White Bear had a gentle, kind manner; he did not seem at all fierce.

The lass thought about the Bear's request for several days. She made up her mind that when the Bear came back, she would go off with him. And neither her father nor her mother could talk her out of it.

When the Bear returned in exactly one week, the lass answered his knock and said she was ready to go with him. She said farewell to her family, climbed onto his shaggy back, and off they went.

"Are you afraid?" asked the White Bear.

"No, not at all," said the lass.

"There is nothing to fear," said the White Bear. "Hold tight to my fur and you won't fall off."

They traveled this way for a long time, until at last they came to a steep cliff. The White Bear knocked on the rocky face of the cliff, and a door opened for them.

Inside was a fine castle of many rooms, all brightly lit and richly furnished. The Bear led the way to a room where a table was laid and supper waiting. Then he gave the lass a small silver bell. Whenever she wanted anything, said the Bear, she was to ring the bell, and it would be brought to her. The lass thanked him, and the Bear left.

The lass was very hungry, so she ate the supper. Then, very sleepy from her long journey, she found a bedchamber and went to sleep.

She lived cheerfully in the castle under the hill for some months. Her only companion all this time was the White Bear, and as time went on she became quite fond of him. But although he talked with her quite gaily, he would answer no questions about either the castle or himself.

Only one thing troubled her. At night, just as she was falling asleep, she would hear someone come into the room and lie down. In the morning, when she awoke, there was no one to be seen. She puzzled over this for some time, wondering if it was the White Bear who came into the room—or perhaps a strange underground creature of some kind.

She grew silent thinking about it. The White Bear, noticing her silence, said, "Lass, this castle and all that is in it are yours. I wish you could be happy here! The silver bell will bring you anything you want. Ask me no questions, trust me, and nothing shall harm you."

"I do trust you," said the lass.

"Are you tired of my company?" asked the White Bear sadly. "Do you wish me to go away?"

"No," said the lass warmly. "I have become very fond of you."

But she became more and more curious about the creature who came into her room at night. Since she could ask no questions, she resolved to find out for herself.

The next night she stayed awake until she heard the creature come into the room and fall deeply asleep. Then she got up and lit a candle.

When she brought the candle over to gaze down at the sleeping figure, she could scarcely believe her eyes! It was a young man with fair hair and a pleasant, open face. As she gazed in surprise, three drops of hot tallow fell from the candle onto his white shirt. The young man woke up.

He stared at her in sorrow. "Oh, lass, what you have done will bring grief to us both! A wicked troll has bewitched me so that I am a White Bear by day and a man by night. There is only one way for me to break the enchantment. If you had willingly stayed with me a full year without knowing my true form, I would be freed. Now that you have seen me, I am still in their power."

"Surely there is something I can do to save you?" cried the lass.

He shook his head. "I must leave you now to return to the Land of the Trolls."

"Can I come with you?" she asked. "I am not afraid."

But again he shook his head.

"Tell me the way, then, and I will search for you until I find you."

He looked at her with gratitude and love. "I'm afraid you will never find that place. Few mortals can. It lies East of the Sun and West of the Moon, and there is no road that leads to it."

Before he could say anything more, both the man and the castle disappeared. The lass found herself sitting in the middle of a forest, dressed in the ragged clothes she had worn when she first met the White Bear.

"I failed to help the White Bear break the enchantment," she thought, "but if I seek him out in the Land of the Trolls I may be able to help him escape their power."

So she started off and walked many weary days, asking everyone she met, "Can you tell me the way to the place that lies East of the Sun and West of the Moon?"

But no one had ever heard of the place, until one day she met an old woman who said kindly, "I have heard that a prince is held prisoner in a castle that lies East of the Sun and West of the Moon. How to get there I do not know. Ask the East Wind."

The lass walked and walked until she reached the home of the

East Wind. There she asked if the East Wind knew the way to the castle East of the Sun, West of the Moon.

"I have heard of it," said the East Wind, "but I don't know the way. I have never blown so far. Perhaps the West Wind knows. I will carry you there, lass."

With a gentle swoop she was lifted up into the air and carried along over the earth to the home of the West Wind.

"This lass seeks the prince in the castle East of the Sun and West of the Moon," said the East Wind. "Do you know where it is?"

"No," said the West Wind, "I have never blown that far. I will take her to the South Wind, who has traveled over more lands than we have."

With a brisk flurry the West Wind took her up into the clouds and carried her along swiftly.

"Are you afraid?" called the West Wind.

"Not at all," said the lass.

When at last they reached the home of the South Wind, the West Wind told of the lass's quest.

"I've blown over many lands," said the South Wind, "but I've not seen such a place. I'll take the lass to the North Wind. The North Wind is the oldest and strongest of us. If the North Wind does not know where it is, it cannot be found!"

The South Wind lifted her high above the earth and carried her along on a strong, steady breeze until they reached the cold home of the North Wind.

"What do you want?" roared the North Wind.

"You needn't be so cross!" said the South Wind. "I have a brave lass here who seeks the prince in the castle East of the Sun, West of the Moon. Have you ever been there?"

"I know where it is," said the North Wind. "It's a great distance. I blew an aspen leaf there once, and I was so tired I had to rest before I could return."

"Can you tell me the way?" asked the lass. "I will go myself."

"No need for that," growled the North Wind. "If you are not afraid to come with me, I'll carry you there."

"I'm not afraid," said the lass. "I will go with you, thank you, for I must get there as fast as I can."

The North Wind blew hard, and with a roar they shot up into the air high above the land and the seas. They raced along, the North Wind blowing with all its power. Down below, a storm raged. Trees were uprooted, and on the sea, ships tossed madly. They tore on and on over the sea until even the powerful North Wind became weaker and weaker. They dropped down lower and lower over the crests of the waves. The icy spray splashed her legs.

"Are you afraid?" puffed the North Wind.

"No, I am not afraid," she replied. But she was glad to see the outline of land ahead.

With a final burst of strength, the North Wind dropped her on the shore close to the castle that lay East of the Sun and West of the Moon.

"I must rest a day on the shore," puffed the North Wind faintly. "This is no place for a lass. Are you sure you want to stay?"

The lass said she must free the prince if she could. So she thanked the North Wind and went on her way.

Since it was still daylight, there was not a troll to be seen. She walked to the castle and sat down near the gates to think of how she could free the prince.

As soon as the sun went down, out came the trolls, hairy, red-eyed creatures scurrying about chattering and shrieking to one another in great excitement. The sight of them was enough to scare the bravest mortal.

But the lass had come this far in her quest, and she would not hesitate now. Gathering her courage, she walked boldly up to one of the troll women.

"Can you tell me what is going on?" she asked politely. "Is there some work I could do for a night's lodging and a bit of food?"

"Tonight is the night the prince must choose a bride from among us!" cried the troll woman exultantly. "When the moon stands high over the treetops, we meet in that clearing by the old oak—and the one who can wash the three spots of tallow from his shirt can claim the prince!"

The troll woman shrieked with glee as she hurried off after the others. Trolls were coming to the clearing from all directions, so the lass followed them.

In the clearing was a large pot of water, and in front of it sat rows of chattering trolls. When the moon stood high above the treetops, the prince came with his shirt. He looked about at the throng of trolls and grew pale. But when he saw the lass standing alone at the rear of the crowd, he smiled in relief.

"Now we'll begin," said a troll woman who seemed to be their leader. And she began very confidently to wash the shirt. But the more she rubbed and scrubbed, the bigger the spots grew.

"Ha!" cried another troll woman. "It's clear you cannot wash the shirt clean. You can never claim the prince. Let me try!"

She seized the shirt and went to work. But she did no better. Her scrubbing and rubbing only made the spots bigger and darker.

All the trolls clamored to wash the shirt. They took turns, grabbing it from one another, each troll scrubbing away with her claws as hard as she could. The shirt only looked darker and dirtier than ever. The three tallow spots did not come out. By now the night was ending.

"You have all tried, and none of you can wash the tallow spots off!" cried the prince. "I see a beggar lass standing there. I'm sure she knows how to wash the shirt! Come here, lass," he called.

The lass went to him quickly.

"Can you wash the shirt clean?" he asked.

"I don't know," she said. "I can try."

She took the shirt to the large cauldron of water and dipped the shirt down into it. At once the shirt became clean and white. When she took the shirt out of the water, the tallow spots were gone.

"Yes," said the prince, smiling, "that proves you are the lass for me!"

The pack of trolls shrieked in disappointed rage. They scrambled to their feet to attack, but the prince clasped hands with the lass and ran for the shore.

At that moment the sun came up. The trolls, trapped by daylight, turned to stone, where they stand to this day.

As for the prince and the lass—the North Wind, with a strong gust, lifted them high above the sea and carried them back to their own country.

THE HUNTER
MAIDEN

A Zuni Tale from the American Southwest

. . .

*L*ong ago, among the Zuni people in the South-
west, there lived a young Indian maiden. She lived alone with her
aged parents in their pueblo. Her two brothers had been killed in
warfare, and it was her responsibility to supply the family with
food and firewood.

The little family lived very simply. During the summer, when
the girl grew beans, pumpkins, squash, melon, and corn in their
garden, they had enough to eat. But when cold weather came, there
were only dried beans and corn to feed the family.

The Zuni people did not graze sheep and cattle in those days; to
keep hunger at bay through the winter, they had to hunt game. Her
brothers' stone axes and rabbit sticks for hunting hung on the walls

unused—for it was the custom that only men could hunt, and her father had grown too old and feeble for hunting.

One year the cold weather set in early and the first snow had fallen. Now was the time the girl must gather brush and firewood to store on the roof of their house.

"We have little to eat," she said to herself, "but at least we will be warm."

As she worked, she watched the young men of the tribe go forth with their rabbit sticks and stone axes. Later in the day, she saw them return to the village with strings of rabbits.

"If I were a boy," she thought, "I could hunt rabbits, and my parents would have meat to nourish them." She pondered this, saying to herself, "There is no reason why *I* can't hunt rabbits. When I was a child, my brothers often took me with them on the hunt."

So that evening, as the girl sat by the fire with her parents, she told them she intended to hunt for rabbits the next day.

"It will not be hard to track rabbits in the new snow," she said. "The young men who went out this morning all returned with strings of rabbits—but we have nothing to barter for meat. The rabbit sticks and axes of my brothers are on the wall. Why should I not use them? Must we go hungry again this winter?"

Her mother shook her head. "No, no! You will be too cold. You will lose your way in the mountains."

"It would be too dangerous," said her father. "It is better to live with hunger. Hunting is not women's work."

But at last, seeing that the girl was determined to go, the old father said, "Very well! If we cannot persuade you against it, I will see what I can do to help you."

He hobbled into the other room and found some old furred deerskins. These he moistened, softened, and cut into long stockings that he sewed up with sinew and the fiber of the yucca leaf. Then he selected for her a number of rabbit sticks and a fine stone ax.

Her mother prepared lunch for the next day, little baked corn-meal cakes flavored with peppers and wild onions. These she strung on a yucca fiber, like beads on a string, and placed with the weapons for the hunt.

The girl rose very early the next morning, for she planned to leave before the young men of the village set out to hunt. She put on a warm, short-skirted dress, pulled on the deerskin stockings, and threw a large mantle over her back. The string of corn cakes was slung over one shoulder, the rabbit sticks thrust into her belt. Carrying the stone ax, she set out for the river valley beyond their pueblo.

Though the snow lay smooth and unbroken, it was not deep enough to hinder her. Moving along steadily, she came at last to the river valley, where she climbed to the cliffs and canyons on the steep, sloping sides. In and around the rocks and bushes she saw the tracks of many rabbits.

She followed the tracks eagerly, running from one place to another. At first she had little skill. But remembering all that her brothers had showed her, she at last became skillful enough to add many rabbits to her string.

Snow had begun to fall, but the girl did not heed this, nor did she notice that it was growing dark.

"How happy my parents will be to have food! They will grow stronger now," she said to herself. "Some of the meat we can dry to last many days."

The string of rabbits had grown very heavy on her back when she suddenly realized it was almost dark. She looked about her. The snow had wiped out her trail. She had lost her way.

The girl turned and walked in what she thought was the direction of her village—but in the darkness and the strangeness of falling white snow, she became confused. She struggled on until she realized that she was completely lost.

"It is foolish to go on," she thought. "I'll take shelter among the rocks for the night and find my way home in daylight."

As she moved along the rocky cliffside, she saw a very small opening that led into a cave. Crawling in cautiously, she found the cave empty. On the floor of the cave were the remains of a fire, a bed of still-glowing ashes. Had another hunter rested here and then left? Delighted with her good luck, she dropped her string of rabbits and hurried to gather twigs and piñon wood from outside. She brought in several armloads to build up the fire for the night ahead.

Sitting down before the crackling fire, she cleaned one of the rabbits and roasted the meat on a spit. With the remaining corn cakes, this made a fine meal. Afterwards she lay back on the stone floor of the cave, ready for sleep.

Then, from the dark stillness out on the mountain, came a long, drawn-out call. Thinking it someone lost in the snow, the girl went to the mouth of the cave and called, "Here!" in answer.

The crackling and snapping of twigs told her someone was coming nearer. Then she heard the sound of a loud rattle and saw the outline of a huge figure.

"Ho!" called a harsh voice. "So you are in there, are you!"

She stood a moment, frozen in dismay and terror. Huge red eyes glared at her, and she knew it was one of the Cannibal Demons that haunted the world from ancient times. She ran to the back of the cave, crouching down out of sight.

The monstrous Demon was at the mouth of the cave, trying to get in, but the opening was too small for his huge body.

"Let me in!" he roared. "I'm hungry and cold."

The girl did not answer.

Then the Demon called out slyly, "Come out here and bring me something to eat."

"I have nothing for you. I've eaten all my food," the girl answered.

"Bring out the rabbits you caught," he demanded. "I can smell them. I know you have rabbits."

The girl threw out a rabbit. The monster seized it in his long, clawlike hand and swallowed the rabbit in one gulp.

"More!" he demanded.

The girl threw out another rabbit from her string. Again he tossed it into his huge mouth. With a snap of his long, sharp teeth, it went down in one swallow.

"Give me all the rabbits!" he shouted.

Now the girl was angry. "I have no more. Go away!"

The monster swelled with a terrible rage. "I'm coming in there to eat you and your rabbits!"

Again he tried to crawl into the cave, but the opening was too small for even his head to get through. Then he stood up. Lifting his great flint ax, he began to shatter the stones at the entrance. Clatter, pound, crash went the ax on the rocks. Gradually the entrance to the cave became a little larger.

The loud crash of the flint ax on rock traveled clearly through the night air. Far away, on Thunder Mountain, two War Gods heard it. They knew at once that it was the Cannibal Demon's ax, and they knew he was again causing trouble.

Picking up their weapons, they flew through the darkness to the cliffside where the Demon hammered away at the cave entrance. They understood the situation at a glance. Each one swung his war club and hit the Demon on the head. The monster fell to the ground, dead.

"You are safe now, maiden," they called. "We will sleep out here at the entrance to your cave and protect you until morning."

The next day as the sun rose, sparkling the white snow, the girl came out of the cave with her string of rabbits. The two War Gods praised her strength and courage. Then they walked with her down the snow-covered valley to guide her to her village. As they traveled through the fresh new whiteness of the world, the two War Gods taught the maiden much hunting wisdom.

When they could see the pueblo in the far distance, the girl turned to her two companions, bowing low and breathing on their hands to thank them. When she straightened up, they had disappeared.

The girl walked into the village, proudly carrying her string of rabbits. All the people stared at her in wonder. Never had they seen a maiden hunter, and the number of rabbits she had caught astonished them. She did not stop, but hurried on to her own home.

When she entered, her parents cried out in joy to see her unharmed. They feared she had been eaten by a mountain lion.

"Now we have food to eat," she cried. "I'll cook a fine rabbit stew to make you strong. And there will be furs for the bitter cold of winter."

"You have done well, daughter . . . and hunter maiden," her father added, smiling. "From now on you will hunt for our family, and your brothers' axes will be yours."

THE GIANT'S DAUGHTER

A Scandinavian Tale

• • •

$\mathbb{A}$ long time ago, giants and trolls dwelt in the high mountain forests above the northern fjords. They kept to themselves and had little to do with the people who lived in the valley below—except to scare the wits out of one of them now and then.

Gina was different; she was quite curious about the humans living in the little houses down in the valley and along the shore. Of course she was still young, as giants go, and not fully grown. That would explain her foolishness, thought her father.

"She has the curiosity of a bear cub," grumbled her mother, "but it's very unnatural to bother with humankind."

"Have nothing to do with people," advised the elder giants.

"Small, stupid creatures! Frightened by a boulder thrown or a sheep carried off!"

Nonetheless, on clear days young Gina would sit on a rock at the lower edge of the forest, watching the people below go about their daily work. It seemed to Gina that these people had a splendid time; the maidservants especially caught her attention, moving about from dairy to stream, laughing together as they worked.

"The work is so easy, I could do it with one hand," thought she. "And so many kinds of food just for the taking!" Gina, it must be admitted, was just a little greedy. She loved to eat.

She was also quite stubborn. Once she had made up her mind to go down to the village below, no one could dissuade her.

Her cousins, the mountain trolls, shrilled, "But they are our enemy! You will be killed, and it will serve you right."

"You foolish child," cried her mother in alarm. "Mark my words, there will be trouble. No good will come of it."

"No good will come of it!" warned the uncles, the aunts, and all the rest of the giants.

But they were all quite wrong.

One day Gina, hop-skipping over the boulders, came down the mountain to the village. At the first two houses where she stopped to ask for work, she had no luck at all.

At the third house, the mistress looked at the very tall, strongly built girl with the large round head and thought, "Here's a bargain indeed! An odd-looking country girl, but she'll do very well for chopping wood and pounding the wash." She told Gina to come in.

Gina bent down, ducking her head to enter the house. "Such queer, tiny houses," thought she. "Doorways much too small, roofs much too low for comfort."

Gina was set to work at once, but it was not many days before the mistress regretted having taken in the strange girl. Gina chopped wood with a will, but so violently that the chunks flew in all directions—one struck a rooster stone dead; one sent a dog yowling off in surprise; another whacked a cart horse so sharply that he bolted off, spilling rounds of cheese right and left. Then she carried such huge armloads of wood into the house that the door burst off its hinges.

Set to work with a tub of wash at the stream, she pounded the laundry so thoroughly that all the clothes and linens came out in rags. To make matters worse, Gina ate more than all the other servants put together. Even between meals she found her way into the storeroom and sat happily devouring jars of honey, vats of pickles, and long strings of sausages.

The mistress brought this tale of woe to her husband, a merchant. "She is impossible!" cried the mistress. "We must get rid of her. When she scours pots, she grinds holes in them! When she washes dishes, she breaks half of them! If she sits on my chairs, they collapse. No, I can't keep her a day longer; she'll be the ruin of us!"

But if Gina was greedy about food, the merchant was miserly about money. "She's powerfully strong and we pay her no wages," he pointed out to his wife—for Gina knew nothing of money or wages. "We could never get a village girl to work for us without payment. And where could we find one half so strong? Gina's twice as strong as a man. I'll find work for her."

So although the mistress complained bitterly about the havoc Gina caused and wanted to get rid of her at once, the merchant insisted she be kept on.

He set Gina to heavy outdoor work, carrying bales of hay to the barn. But Gina thought it fun to toss the bales into the hayloft, and if she knocked down a farmhand in the process, she merely roared with laughter. If a horse kicked her, she gave the animal a powerful kick right back. All this caused such an uproar in the barnyard that the merchant quickly set Gina to unloading the fishing boats that came to his wharf. Here she did the work of two or three men.

Delighted with such a strong and willing worker, the merchant used Gina everywhere—from sausage and cheese making to building a new storage barn. In the new barn he had Gina build a room and bed of her own, for the mistress declared that she was not fit to live in a house. The merchant, however, rubbed his hands in satisfaction thinking of the money he saved.

And what about Gina? Gina was enjoying herself. The heavy work did not bother her at all. She joined in the village dances, but she swung her partners with such vigor that they whirled away across the field. After that, partners were hard to find. Still, everything new fascinated her. Although she thought humans most peculiar in their ways, she marveled at their cleverness.

Their houses were too small, their furniture too flimsy, but it was fine to sleep on a bed instead of a pile of leaves, or use an ax to chop wood instead of breaking it apart with her hands. And to think one might keep chickens to have eggs whenever one wished! Her sharp, inquisitive eyes took in everything that went on around her.

Things went on in this way for several months. But while the merchant became more and more pleased with his bargain, the mistress became more and more irritated with Gina. She determined to get rid of her.

In the spring, the merchant prepared to sail down to Bergen on a trading voyage. His wife announced that she would go with him. Just before they set sail, she took Gina aside and said sharply, "I don't want to find you here when we return. I advise you to go back to wherever you came from!"

Then she quickly joined her husband aboard the ship, and they sailed away down the fjord with a stiff breeze. Gina was left on shore with the village folk who had turned out to see the merchant off. Next to her stood two maidservants from the village.

"Wish you were going with them?" said one. "Save the money they pay you, Gina, and you can go to Bergen yourself someday!"

"Money they pay me?" repeated Gina in surprise.

"Your wages for working," said the other. "I noticed you never spend any money. You must have a nice little sum hidden away!"

"They never gave me any money for working!"

The two girls laughed at her. "Oh you *are* a green one! You worked almost a year for nothing?"

"Greedy old man," said the other. "No wonder he's so rich!"

When Gina finally understood that all the other country girls were paid, her eyes became quite red with anger. She stalked back to the merchant's place. There she sat down and thought for a long time.

"Payment I shall have," she said finally. "I'll take it myself!"

At once she set to work. She pulled out an old cart from the barn and loaded it with all the things she had decided to take with her. In went a cock and a hen, an ax, nails—she knew what she needed for the success of her plan. And when the cart was filled, she didn't forget to toss in a round wheel of cheese, a crock of pickles, and several strings of her favorite sausages.

Then she pulled the loaded cart up the mountain until she reached the high pine forests, the land of the trolls and giants.

Swinging the ax with gusto, she soon converted trees into the framework of a tall one-room house. She made sure that the doorway was big and wide and the roof high enough for a full-grown giant. Next to it was a fenced-in yard for the cock and hen.

From time to time the giants and trolls came by to watch her work and to gape in astonishment at so much mad activity.

"Poor Gina," they said to each other. "She's become as crazy as a loon, living with humans all that time. I knew no good would come of it!"

"She'll never marry now," lamented Gina's mother. "She's collected no fur pelts for dowry. What sensible giant would want that pile of wood?"

But again they were all quite wrong.

When Gina had finished all her work, the first frost sparkled on the ground, and the smell of snow was in the air. She now had a tall house made of logs, snug against the winter cold. She had an open hearth and a stack of firewood; a big, solid chair; a large bed covered with fur pelts; chickens safely housed in a lean-to; rounds of cheese made from wild goat and reindeer milk; sausages and wild boar hams hanging from the rafters.

By the time the heavy snow had settled on the mountain, even the sour trolls had to admit that the warm log house was better than a cave or a deep underground hole. It dawned on the folk of the forest that Gina was not crazy at all. She was in fact very clever.

And what better dowry could a young giant girl have than a snug hut and strings of fragrant sausages? All the giant folk now called her Clever Gina, and as the winter thawed into Spring, Gina was besieged with offers to marry.

"Perhaps I'll marry, or perhaps I won't," she said carelessly. "I'll think about it." And since the young giants were very eager to bring her rabbits or wild boar and other game in exchange for eggs, cheese, or the loan of her ax, it seemed to Gina that "thinking about it" was a very good arrangement indeed.

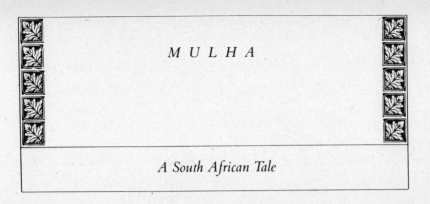

MULHA

A South African Tale

. . .

Long ago in southern Africa, demon spirits and monstrous ogres were much more to be feared than the wild animals of the forests. The ogres were both sly and cruel—they could quickly change their shapes, and were said to devour children.

Mulha, like many other children, had heard tales of the ogre Inzimu and his sister Imbula. However, it was not until she was fourteen and almost fully grown that she came face to face with these monsters. This is the way it happened:

One day Mulha's father was away hunting. Her mother was at work tending the crops in their field, some distance away. Mulha's task was to stay at the family's thatched hut and care for her two younger sisters. Unfortunately, Mulha became quite bored watching the children.

Her eyes fell on the large storage pot standing near the door of the hut. The three children had always been forbidden to open this pot, but this day Mulha decided she was going to peek inside. Perhaps, she thought hungrily, her mother kept honey cakes or special food treats there.

So Mulha lifted up the heavy lid. Before she could even see the contents, a small, sharp-fanged animal that had hidden there leaped out and grew at once into a huge ogre. When Mulha saw his long tail, she knew he was the ogre Inzimu.

The three girls ran into the hut, the Inzimu after them.

"I won't harm you," said he, making his voice as sweet as honey. "I only want you to cook me some dinner. I'm very hungry."

He persuaded the two older girls to go out for buckets of water; then, as soon as they left the hut, he popped the youngest girl into a large cooking pot and put on a heavy lid.

While the two girls were filling the buckets, a large honeybee buzzed about their heads. The buzzing became words: "The Inzimu has hidden your little sister in the cooking pot!"

"How can we save her?" cried the younger sister.

Mulha thought a few moments. Then she said, "After we return, I will run out of the hut. As soon as the Inzimu chases me, you must rescue our sister; both of you run into the brush behind the hut and hide."

The girls returned with the water and stood quietly near the door. Suddenly Mulha called out in a taunting voice, "You will never catch *me*, Inzimu!" And she ran out of the hut.

In a rage, the Inzimu started after her. But he tripped over the pail of water the younger sister thrust out, and Mulha had a good start. Fleet as a deer, she dodged among the bushes and trees until she reached the river. There she plunged in and swam easily to the other side—for she knew the Inzimu was powerless to follow her over water.

The Inzimu returned to find the small hut empty, and after shouting angry threats of revenge, he departed. But the younger sisters did not creep out of their hiding place until they heard their parents' return.

After Mulha's parents heard the story of the Inzimu who had hidden in the storage pot, they became very alarmed.

"We must leave this hut," declared the father. "Our children are not safe here. The Inzimu will surely return another day. We will go down the valley to my brother's house."

Quickly the family packed up their possessions and left.

"The Inzimu will try to take revenge on Mulha. It was she who tricked him," said the mother. "We must send her away."

To be sure Mulha would be safe, her parents decided to send her to stay with an older married sister living in a distant kraal. Since this was less than a day's walk, Mulha assured her parents she could follow the track to the kraal alone.

Dressed in her best garment, a gaily striped black cloth knotted about her waist, and wearing her brightest ornaments, Mulha set out with a light step. She promised to be very careful and to remember her mother's warning to eat nothing along the way.

It was midsummer, however, and the afternoon was hot. Soon Mulha became very thirsty. When she saw a manumbela tree covered with ripe berries, she could not resist them. Hitching up her skirt, she climbed the tree, and she ate the juicy berries.

As soon as she returned to the ground, the tree trunk opened. Out came a huge woman, an Imbula, with an ugly animal snout and a hairy red pelt covering her body.

"You are not safe traveling alone," said the Imbula, making her voice as sweet as honey. "You will be robbed of all your pretty things. I will go with you to protect you—but first we must exchange clothes so that you will be safe."

Mulha protested in vain; the Imbula promised to return everything to Mulha when they approached the kraal. Then she pulled off Mulha's skirt, and in no time at all she had forced the exchange of clothing.

To her horror, Mulha found that the red, hairy pelt of the Imbula clung to her tightly, as if it were her own skin. The Imbula, wearing Mulha's skirt and ornaments, now looked exactly like Mulha, while Mulha had become an ugly monster!

Not knowing what else to do, Mulha followed the Imbula along the trail. When they approached the kraal, Mulha cried, "Now give me back my clothes!"

Not only did the Imbula refuse, but she walked in through the gate of the kraal with great assurance and asked for her married sister. The sister welcomed the false Mulha warmly.

"What shall we do with this strange creature with you?" asked the married sister, wrinkling her nose in distaste.

"Put her away in an old hut; she can eat with the dogs," said the Imbula. "It's all she's fit for."

So Mulha, whom her parents had thought the prettiest maiden in Swaziland, was sent to a wretched hut to live with a poor old woman. The Imbula, seemingly a pretty maiden, was made much of by the people in the village. The false Mulha had just one problem: all Imbulas have tails, as Inzimus do, and this she could not get rid of. She had managed to wind hers around and around her waist, where it was hidden by her clothing. Each day she feared it would be discovered, but for a time all went well for the Imbula.

Meanwhile, the real Mulha lived as an outcast in the hut of the old woman. But she did not waste time crying over the cruel revenge taken by the Inzimu and the Imbula. She quickly discovered that the ugly, hairy pelt she wore gave her some magic power; she could obtain choice food simply by commanding it. So, with the old woman sworn to secrecy, the two ate well and lived quietly together in comfort.

Almost every day, Mulha went down early to a deserted part of the river to bathe. As soon as she entered the water, the hairy skin floated away, and she became her own self. She swam happily about for a while, but as she left the water, the skin attached itself to her again, and she became the strange creature as before.

One day the married sister went down to the river to wash some clothes. Catching sight of the strange, hairy woman at the water's edge, she hid herself and watched. What she saw astonished her. She hurried home at once to consult the chief's aging sister, who was well known for her wisdom.

The next time the creature went to bathe, the two women hid near the riverbank. They saw the ugly pelt float away while Mulha swam, and attach itself when she left the water.

The two women confronted Mulha, demanding an explanation. She told them she was the real Mulha, and explained how she had been tricked by the Imbula.

"If you really are Mulha and the other is not, surely you can prove it!" said the married sister. But it was clear she was not certain in her mind that this was her sister, and Mulha was hurt.

"Why bother with me?" said Mulha. "You took the Imbula in as your sister; now you can keep her! I have everything I want. Only more trouble will come to me if I accuse the Imbula."

"The girl is right," said the chief's sister. "The Imbula still has power to do her harm. She may take further revenge because Mulha outwitted her brother, the Inzimu. Come away now," said she to the married sister. "We will consult with my brother the chief and devise a plan. For the true Imbula must be discovered and killed if Mulha is to be saved."

A few days later a big hole was dug in the middle of the kraal. In it were placed food and a large calabash filled with fresh milk. Each woman in the kraal was commanded to walk all around the hole by herself.

At last came the turn of the Imbula. She begged to be excused. "I am too shy a maiden to walk about before all the people," said she in a tiny, sweet voice. This did not help her at all.

The chief and his sister forced her to begin the walk around the hole. At the sight of the fresh white milk, her Imbula nature could not be controlled. Of its own accord, her tail uncoiled and slithered down into the hole to suck up the milk—for no Inzimu or Imbula can control its tail when milk is on the ground! The chief's sister had known this when she devised the trap.

With a shriek of rage at her unmasking, the Imbula seized a child nearby and leaped toward the gate. But the hunters were waiting with spears ready, and she was slain. The moment the Imbula was killed, Mulha regained her own true form.

After that, Mulha lived peacefully with her sister's family. Eventually she married the chief's youngest son. The one hundred cows paid to Mulha's father as the bride price made it possible for her family to live in great comfort.

And that was how Mulha outwitted the ogre Inzimu and, with the help of the chief's sister, escaped the Imbula's revenge.

ELSA AND THE EVIL WIZARD

A Swedish Tale

· · ·

*L*ong, long ago, a very evil wizard lived in a splendid castle high in the mountains. Outside the castle were large, beautiful gardens filled with bright flowers and delicious fruits.

Scattered throughout the gardens were statues of young maidens so perfect that one would think them alive. And it was a sad fact that once these statues had been living maidens. For whenever the wizard saw a young maid who took his fancy, he would cleverly seize her and fly away with her to his castle. There the wizard turned the girl into a stone statue to adorn his gardens.

Whenever he tired of gazing at his collection of statues, he made ready to fly off in search of a new victim. He put on the fine clothes of a nobleman and rubbed his lips with honey to make his voice sweet and beguiling. He sprinkled his cruel face with May morning dew to make it look gentle and kind. Then he wrapped himself in his magic flying cloak. The cloak changed at once to large dark wings, and he flew out over the cliffs and dark pine forests. He circled and dipped, flying lower and lower over the valleys.

If he saw someone he fancied, he would spread his dark cloak on the ground. If a maiden but stepped onto it—even the edge—he would seize her and carry her off. But the wizard's power was not absolute. Unless the victim willingly stepped onto the cloak, he had no power to harm her.

One morning the evil wizard circled and coasted above the valleys longer than usual, for he had a fancy to seek a maiden with long golden hair. At last he saw Elsa walking along a path outside the village, with a berry basket on her arm. Her long yellow hair glistened in the sunlight as she bent now and then to pick raspberries.

The gleaming gold drew him downward. He was enchanted. What a fine new statue he would have for his garden! He floated to the ground and took cover behind a clump of hawthorn.

When Elsa drew near, he stepped out and spread his cloak on the path.

"Beautiful maiden," he said, bowing low, "allow me to be of service. Your feet are too dainty and tender to walk on rough, muddy ground. Step onto my cloak."

Elsa laughed. "I'm not a beautiful maiden, and my feet are quite sturdy, thank you! You should take better care of your cloak. How foolish to drop it onto the path! It will be covered with mud."

She picked up the cloak, shook off the dirt, and handed it to the wizard. "You'll ruin your fine cloak, throwing it on the ground for girls to walk on!" With a cheerful smile and a nod, she walked briskly on.

The wizard frowned. He followed behind her at a short distance, wondering how he could trap her.

Some distance ahead he saw a herd of goats grazing, and among them a powerful billy goat with sharp horns.

"If I make the goat attack her," he thought, "she will run to me for protection. Surely then she will step on the edge of my cloak."

He blew on his magic whistle to attract a swarm of bees. They stung the billy goat about the face. Enraged, the goat tried in vain to butt the bees. Then he caught sight of Elsa. Lowering his horns, he rushed to attack her.

The wizard ran forward with his outspread cloak trailing on the ground. "I will protect you!" he cried.

But Elsa ignored him. She darted behind a bush, the goat after her. Around and around the bush they ran.

The wizard stood by, vexed, waving the cloak with little effect, until Elsa tripped. He quickly threw the cloak down, expecting that she would fall on it. But Elsa rolled to one side, and it was the goat who became tangled in the cloak.

With a blow of his fist, the wizard knocked the goat senseless. Then he angrily pulled his cloak from the horns. The cloak came free, but it had a large rip in it.

When Elsa saw the torn cloak, she felt sorry for him. "Your fine cloak is torn, and all because you tried to protect me," she said kindly. "I'll see what I can do to mend it."

She picked a thin sharp thorn from a hawthorn bush and, with another sharp thorn, pierced a small hole in the top to make a needle. Then she took a strand of her long yellow hair to use as a thread.

"Hand me your cloak, sir. I will sew the tear as neatly as I can." She sat down, holding the cloak on her knee, and sewed up the tear with the strand of golden hair.

The wizard was not the least bit grateful. When Elsa handed him the cloak, he shook it out to examine it and complained that the tear needed more stitches. "Look here, how loosely you've sewn it!"

As Elsa moved closer to look, the wizard trailed the corner of the cloak on the ground. Elsa's foot stepped onto the hem!

In an instant, both Elsa and the wizard were wrapped in the cloak. The wizard's face changed to become a face of evil—his eyes were glowing red balls, his cruel mouth showed long yellow teeth, and his arm gripped Elsa's waist. The large dark wings of the cloak spread outward, and Elsa found they were moving upward into the air.

But the strand of yellow hair she had used to sew the cloak caught on a branch of a tree. There it held them fast and did not break.

Try as he would, the wizard could not free them. The more he pulled and tugged, the more the cloak became tangled in the branches. At last, with an angry curse, he used his two hands to pull at the cloak. Freed from his grip, Elsa slid to a lower branch and from there leaped to the ground.

She raced back over the path toward the village and home. Never in her life had she run so fast! She didn't stop until she reached her room and fell upon her bed in complete exhaustion. When she could speak, she told her widowed mother all that had happened.

The wizard flew back to his castle in a terrible rage. He slammed doors, hurled his silver jug across the room to break a mirror, and stormed about the castle so viciously that all his servants hid from him.

That night he lay down on his bed, but he found he could not sleep. The room was strangely bright, and the light hurt his eyes.

"The moon is shining through the window," he thought. But

when he got up to close the shutters on the window, he saw there was no moon in the sky. The bright light was within the room.

Then he saw that the light came from his cloak, which was lying over a chair. The stitches of the mended tear, sewn with Elsa's golden hair, glowed brilliantly against the dark cloak, filling the room with a very bright light.

"Ho!" said he. "So that's the way of it! The stitches will be easy to hide." He rolled the cloak up tightly, with the mended seam inside, and went back to bed.

But again the bright radiance filled the room, shining through the folds of cloth.

"That blasted girl and her golden hair!" he shouted in rage.

He ran down to the castle cellars and hid his cloak under a barrel. It did not help a bit. As soon as he wearily climbed the stairs and fell into bed again, the bright light glowed through all the castle rooms, right up to his bedroom. He was unable to sleep all night.

The next evening his room again glowed with light. He brought the cloak up from the cellars and, with a knife, tried to cut the golden stitches. But he could not cut them.

"Stupid, silly girl!" he kept muttering to himself. "Sewing up *my* cloak with her nasty hair!" In a frenzy, he slashed the mended seam right out of his cloak, leaving a large hole. Then he threw the piece out of the window and went to bed.

But again the brilliant light filled the room. He got out of bed and ran to look at his cloak. The mended tear was back in place, the golden thread still shining brightly.

He knew at last that he had no power to get rid of Elsa's seam.

He did not sleep that night or the next night or the next. After a week he could stand it no longer. He seized his cloak and flew down to the village where Elsa lived. He peered into one window after another until he found her room. He rapped sharply on her window.

Elsa sat up in bed in surprise. "Who's that?"

"It's me. Open your window and talk to me. I won't hurt you."
Elsa recognized the evil voice. She shivered but did not answer.

"Come here, you wicked girl," he cried. "Take your thread
out of my cloak. It shines with a horrid bright light and won't let
me sleep."

"I will not come to the window," Elsa said. "Go away!"

"I can't sleep, I tell you. For seven nights I've had no sleep! Come,
take out your silly hair from my cloak or I'll make you suffer!"

But Elsa's mother had told her the village lore about the evil
wizard on the mountain. She knew his only power over her lay in
his magic cloak.

When the wizard saw he could not frighten Elsa, he tried another way. "If you take out your thread of hair, I'll give you a sack
of gold," he coaxed.

"I don't want your sack of gold," said Elsa.

"I'll give you a large farm filled with sheep as well,"
he urged.

"I don't want your farm," said Elsa. She didn't trust the wizard
an inch. In desperation the wizard offered one fine thing after
another. Nothing would make Elsa come to the window.

At last he gave up and returned to his castle in a very bad temper.
There he sulked in his garden all the next day, scowling at his stone
statues. The statues stared back sadly.

"That silly, stubborn girl has no fear of me," he thought. "What
can I do to demonstrate my power?" And he conceived the idea of
restoring one of his stone statues to life.

As he watched the released maiden run down the mountain path
to her home, he thought smugly, "That will show the foolish Elsa I
am not to be trifled with!"

That night the brilliant light dimmed, and he was able to sleep.

But the next night the light from the golden stitches returned as bright as ever.

He flew down to Elsa's window in a rage and rapped sharply to waken her.

"Who's that?" called Elsa sleepily.

"You know very well who it is," he cried. "I've had enough of this nonsense! Don't you know I have powers of enchantment far stronger than your stupid hair? You've had your revenge. Now be a sensible girl and remove the seam."

"I think the seam does very well where it is," said Elsa. And no matter how he blustered or threatened, she would say nothing more.

The wizard flew back to his castle on the mountain. There the bright, piercing light from Elsa's seam would not let him sleep until he restored another of the enchanted stone statues to life.

And so, one at a time, he was forced to free the maidens. Each day that he angrily released a maiden from his garden, the strange light faded, and he slept soundly.

When the last statue was gone, Elsa's golden stitches retained a faint, steady glow—enough to warn the wizard that they would flare up brilliantly if he ever used his evil powers again.

MARIA MOREVNA

A Russian Tale

• • •

*L*ong, long ago, when the land of Russia was made up of many small kingdoms, there lived a warrior princess named Maria Morevna.

She had inherited her kingdom from her father, and her father, very wisely, had trained her not only to govern well, but also to defend the kingdom against enemy armies. Many princes sought to marry her, thinking to gain control of the country. Maria Morevna refused them all.

One day the young Prince Alexey rode in from the south and said he wished to serve in the army of Maria Morevna. The long and the short of it was—they fell in love, and the marriage took place three months later at the palace, amid great rejoicing.

The young couple lived happily together for one year.

Then one day an exhausted messenger rode into the palace courtyard to bring tidings of an enemy attack on the western borders. While the army assembled for war, Maria sat down with Alexey.

"You will rule here in my absence," she told him. "But, dear Alexey, you must never open the door at the top of the east tower."

After a fond farewell, Maria, splendid in her white and gold uniform, rode off at the head of her army.

Now, Alexey was consumed with curiosity about the door that must not be opened. He resisted for one day. He resisted for two days. But on the third day he weakened and said to himself, "I'll just take a quick look. Surely that can do no harm."

So he climbed the stairs to the tower. Trying each of the keys entrusted to him until he found the one that unlocked the door, he pushed it open and stepped into the room.

He stood rooted to the floor in astonishment—for inside was a tall old man with white hair and a long white beard, who stood chained to the wall.

"I am so weak," cried the old man. "Kind youth, will you bring me a jar of water?"

Alexey felt pity for him. He ran down the steps and filled a large jar with water. When he brought it in, the prisoner drank it down in one gulp.

"I feel stronger," said the old man. "Bring me more water, I beg of you."

And Alexey brought him another full jar of water. This too he gulped down in an instant.

"One more, kind youth," the old man beseeched. Alexey hesitated.

"Bring me one more jar of water, and I promise you I will give you your life when otherwise you must die."

Alexey brought him the third jar of water.

After the prisoner had drained that in a gulp, he swelled in size. As his body grew huge and powerful, his face became cruel and savage. With a quick wrench he broke the heavy iron chains as if they were paper.

"Who are you?" cried Alexey.

"I am Koschei the Wizard," answered the old man exultantly. "Many years ago, the father of Maria Morevna captured me, thinking to rid the country of evil. He destroyed my power and chained me here. Now you have set me free!"

With a swirl of his long cape he flew out of the window and away. High in the air he flew, like a great bird of prey, till he saw Maria Morevna far below, riding proudly with her army. He swooped down, seized the princess, and flew off with her. He flew over nine times seven kingdoms until he reached his own palace near the sea.

Alexey was crushed with grief. The fate of Maria lay heavily on his heart, for he knew his impulsive carelessness was to blame. While the people of the kingdom mourned their princess, Alexey rode off in search of her.

He traveled many roads for many weeks across many kingdoms before he at last arrived at Koschei's palace. Leaving his horse tethered in the forest, he crept as close as he could. He lay hidden until he saw Koschei ride forth on a powerful black horse. Then he climbed a tree and, from an outspread branch, dropped down into the palace garden. There he found Maria Morevna.

They embraced joyfully. But after a moment Maria drew back. "Oh Alexey, why did you disobey my command?" she cried. "Why did you open the room and free the wizard?"

"I was foolish and thoughtless," said Alexey sadly. "I know it has caused you much grief. But if you can forgive the past, we will set off at once. My horse waits in the forest nearby."

"If it were that easy to escape the wizard, I wouldn't be here now," replied Maria. "He possesses a miraculous horse, and he will catch up with us in a trice!"

"I saw him leave for a day's hunting," urged Alexey. "We can be far away before he discovers you are gone."

But Maria cried, "He will kill you if he catches us—and that I could not bear!"

At last Alexey persuaded Maria to try to escape, for he said he would rather be slain than live without her. So, making their way out of the garden, they mounted Alexey's horse and rode off as fast as the steed could carry them.

In the midst of the hunt, some distance away, Koschei's great horse suddenly stopped in its tracks.

"What ails you, you lazy beast?" cried Koschei, bringing down his whip on the horse's flank.

"Prince Alexey has come and carried off Maria Morevna," said the horse.

Koschei swelled with anger. "After them, you stupid nag!" His spurs dug into the horse cruelly, for he, like many with violent tempers, took out his rage on those who served him.

The horse fairly flew over the ground, scarcely needing the whip and spurs of Koschei. Within a very short time they had overtaken Alexey and Maria.

Seizing Alexey under one arm, and Maria under the other, the wizard carried them back to the castle.

"You're a fool. You have no more chance of freeing Maria Morevna than you have of seeing your own ears!" he cried, flinging Alexey to the ground. As the wizard swung his sword high, Alexey cried out, "When I gave you the third jar of water, you promised me my life!"

The sword stopped in midair. "Very well," snarled the wizard. "I will not kill you." And he gave orders for Alexey to be put into a large cask. After the top was tightly sealed, the cask was thrown over the cliff into the sea.

Now, it happened the next day that a hawk, an eagle, and a crow, seeing the cask floating in the sea, became curious and pulled it to shore with their beaks and sharp claws. There they picked at it until they tore it apart.

Great was their astonishment when Alexey crawled out, bruised but unharmed.

Alexey thanked them gratefully, but he added in despair, "I am no more able to free Maria Morevna now that I am outside the cask than I was inside it!" Then Alexey told his rescuers all that had happened since he unwittingly freed the wizard.

"It is clear," said the crow, "that Koschei's horse is a hundred times swifter than any other."

"Try as often as you will," said the hawk, "he is sure to overtake you."

"You must try to obtain another horse the equal of the wizard's," said the eagle. "Maria Morevna must find out from Koschei where and how he obtained his."

Alexey thanked them for their counsel and set off on foot for the wizard's castle. Once more he waited for Koschei to leave, then climbed into the garden.

Maria was overjoyed to see Alexey still alive. When he told her the advice of the three birds, she nodded.

"Yes," she said, "Koschei likes to boast of his steed's power. Come back here tomorrow, Alexey; let us pray I will have an answer for you."

That evening, Maria spoke of Koschei's horse with great admiration. Then she went on, "Tell me, wise wizard, where was this marvelous steed foaled?"

"On the shore of the blue sea grazes a most wonderful mare. Every three years the mare bears a colt. He who can snatch the colt from the wolves waiting to seize it, and bring the colt safely away, will possess a steed like mine."

"And did you bravely snatch the colt from the wolves?" asked Maria.

"No, it was not I," the wizard admitted. "Near this place lives an old Baba Yaga who follows the mare and snatches each colt from the wolves. Thus she has a herd of many miraculous horses. I spent three days tending them, and for a reward she gave me a little colt. That colt grew up to become the horse I ride."

"How clever you were to find the Baba Yaga!" cried Maria. "It cannot have been easy."

"Only I have that power," boasted Koschei. "One must cross a river of fire to reach her land. I have in my silver chest here a magic handkerchief." The wizard took out the piece of scarlet silk. "I waved this handkerchief three times to my right side and a strong bridge appeared, a bridge so high that the fire could not touch it. What do you think of that, eh?" And he sat back well pleased with himself.

Maria exclaimed at his power and cleverness. Then, in the night, after the wizard was asleep, she went to the silver chest and removed the handkerchief.

The very next day, when Alexey once again stole into the palace garden, she gave the magic handkerchief to him and told him what Koschei had revealed.

Alexey set off at once on his long journey, traveling over wet, mired roads and dry, dusty roads. He found the river of fire and, using the magic scarlet silk, safely crossed on the high bridge.

Now he had to find the Baba Yaga. The country was empty and desolate. He had walked three days without food or drink when,

weak with hunger, he came upon a bird with her fledglings. One of these he caught.

The mother bird flew round and round him, squawking desperately. "Do not eat my little one," she cried. "If you will set it free, one day I will do a service for you."

Alexey was moved to pity and set the little bird free.

Soon afterward he found a wild beehive. He was about to pull out the honeycomb when the queen bee buzzed about his face, saying, "Prince, do not take the honey. It is food for my subjects. Leave it—and in return, one day I will do you a service."

Alexey left the honey and struggled hungrily on. That evening he came at last to the shore of the blue sea. Here, leaning over the rocks near the shore, he caught a crayfish.

But the crayfish cried out, "Spare my life, prince. Do not eat me, and one day I will do you a service."

Alexey dropped the crayfish back into the water. He went on so tired and hungry he could scarcely walk.

Not long after this he came to the hut of the Baba Yaga. This hut, as you may know, was set up on high stilts that looked like great chicken legs. He climbed the ladder to the hut and entered.

"Health to thee, Grandmother," said he cautiously.

"Health to thee, prince," she answered, staring at him with sharp, dark eyes. "Why do you come to visit me?"

"I come to serve you as herder," said he. "I want to graze your horses so I may earn a colt as payment."

"So that's the way it is, eh?" The Baba Yaga sat silent a moment, her brown wrinkled face neither friendly nor unfriendly. "Why not?" she said at last. "If you tend the horses well, I'll give you a steed fit for a hero. But if you lose even one of them, I'll lop off your head!"

"Hard terms, Grandmother, but I agree."

The Baba Yaga gave him food and drink and a place to sleep in the corner.

The next day the herd was let out of the stables to pasture. At once they raced off in every direction over the wide steppes, and disappeared. It happened in the blink of an eye, even before Alexey could mount his horse. All day he searched, but he could not find them.

Just as he gave way to despair, a great flock of birds filled the sky. The birds found the horses, swooped down, and pecking at them sharply, drove them home to the stables by evening. Alexey's kindness in setting the fledgling bird free had been rewarded!

When the Baba Yaga saw this, she was very angry. Secretly she ordered the herd to disappear into the thick forest the next day.

And so it happened on the second day. The horses disappeared into a dense forest. Alexey followed them, but though he searched the forest all day, he could not find them. Wearily he sat down on a log. "I shall never get the colt as payment," he thought in despair. "And how will I free Maria Morevna?"

Then suddenly a huge swarm of bees filled the air. They easily sought out the horses, buzzing about their faces and stinging their flanks until all of them fled back to the stable.

That night, while Alexey slept, the Baba Yaga berated the horses soundly; she ordered them to go to the sea the next day and swim until they were completely out of sight.

So it happened on the third day. Alexey, who had followed the horses to the shore, saw them swimming rapidly out to sea. In a trice they had disappeared from sight. Disheartened and weary, he sat down on a rock on the shore. His quest for a steed to rescue Maria now seemed hopeless. He wept, and after that he fell asleep.

It was evening when he was awakened by a crayfish nipping at his finger that was trailing in the water. "The creatures of the sea and shore have driven the horses back. They are safe now in the stable," said the crayfish. "I have served you as I promised. Return now, but hide in the stable—for the Baba Yaga will try to trick you. When the Baba Yaga is asleep, take the shabby little colt standing in the corner and go away at once."

Alexey thanked the crayfish joyfully. He returned to hide in the stable; at midnight, while the Baba Yaga was sleeping soundly, he saddled the shabby colt and rode off. Crossing back over the bridge spanning the river of fire, he found a lush green meadow nearby. Here he grazed the colt at sunrise for twelve mornings. By the twelfth morning, the colt had become a huge and powerful steed. With such a horse as this, he covered the roads back to the wizard's castle in hardly more time than is needed to tell of it.

Maria cried out with joy at the sight of Alexey, but little time was spent in talk. They both mounted Alexey's horse and at once rode off with the speed of the wind.

But the wizard's horse once more faithfully reported Maria's escape. Using whip and spurs, Koschei flew after them.

"You lazy bag of bones," shouted Koschei. "Why don't you overtake them?"

"The horse the prince rides is my younger brother," the wizard's horse replied, "but I will try."

Koschei applied the whip more viciously. As they drew closer to Maria and Alexey, the wizard lifted his great sword to strike.

At that moment the steed Alexey rode cried out to the other, "My brother, why do you serve such a cruel and wicked master? Toss him from your back and kick him sharply with your hooves!"

Koschei's horse heeded the advice of his brother. He threw his rider to the ground and lashed out with his hooves so fiercely that the wizard was forced to crawl back painfully to the castle on all fours, and he never emerged again.

Maria mounted Koschei's horse and they returned in triumph to their own kingdom. There they were welcomed with shouts of surprise and thanksgiving.

Very soon after her return, Maria Morevna again mounted Koschei's horse, leading her army forth to rout the invaders in the west. And Koschei's horse served her faithfully ever after.

DUFFY AND THE DEVIL

A Cornish Tale

•   •   •

*I*t happened one time, in the old days, that the squire of the village needed a new housekeeper. His old housekeeper, Jane, had died, and since her eyes had grown dim in her old age, the squire's hall was now in a sad state.

When the squire hired a crew at cider-pressing time, his eye settled on the strong, sturdy figure of Duffy among the women picking apples.

"Are you needing a job?" said the squire as he paid off at the end of the day.

"I am indeed," said Duffy.

"Can you spin and knit and clean and cook?" asked the squire.

"I make the best meat pies in the village," said Duffy, evading a bit of his question, "but I won't muck out the barns and pigsty."

"I have a man for that," said the squire. "Come along tomorrow then, for I need someone to take old Jane's place."

Duffy was very pleased with her luck until she saw the inside of the squire's hall. Cobwebs and dirt were everywhere. And though the squire had many bags of his own wool piled in the storeroom, the spinning wheel was covered with dust. There had been neither yarn spun nor clothing knitted for a long time.

"Well," said he carelessly, "there's a bit of work to do here. But first you must spin some yarn and knit me some socks, for my feet are clear out of these."

"And your vest and britches are in no better state," thought Duffy grimly.

"You can get on with it," said the squire. "I'll be out hunting all the day." And off he went to the stable.

Duffy stood with her hands on her hips, surveying the sad state of the rooms.

"Well," she thought, "I'll clean up a bit, and then I'll make some meat pies."

When the squire returned hungry that night, he happily sniffed the fragrance of meat pies done to a turn. After downing a fair number of them, he stretched out his legs at the hearth.

"My socks now," he said anxiously. "Have you started the spinning of yarn for my socks?"

"Tomorrow," said Duffy.

But the next day when Duffy confronted the huge sacks of wool waiting to be carded and spun, she groaned in dismay. Duffy was a cheerful soul and a good cook, but spinning was not a thing she liked to do—nor had she much skill at it.

"Yarn for the squire's clothes, blankets for the house—there's no end of spinning and knitting to be done!" she exclaimed as she dusted off the spinning wheel in the kitchen. "The devil himself couldn't do it all!"

"Oh, yes I could!" cried a shrill voice. And out from behind the woodpile at the hearth leaped a small, sharp-featured little man with a long tail.

"Ah, Duffy, my dear, there's no need to work your fingers to the bone, carding and spinning and knitting, when all can be had just for the wishing of it."

"Oh, it can?" said Duffy suspiciously.

"Spun yarn as fine and strong as metal, knit socks, vests that will never wear out," said he in a coaxing voice. "Blankets, britches, all for the wishing."

Twirling his tail, the little man grinned and waited while Duffy considered the offer.

"There'll be a price for it, no doubt?"

"Nay, Duffy my dear, not a price, but a bargain between us. All the spinning and knitting you wish for three years, and at the end of that time you come away with me—"

"Humph! Not much of a bargain!" said Duffy.

"Fair's fair. I was going to add," he went on crossly, "that you must come away with me—unless you can guess my name. I always keep my bargains. You have the honest word of a gentleman."

Duffy knew very well that the "gentleman," as he called himself, was a devil. But as she watched the vain little man confidently swinging his tail, she thought, "In three years' time I can get the best of the bargain. It shouldn't be too difficult to find out his name!"

"Agreed," said Duffy.

The little man nodded and grinned—and in the next moment he had disappeared from sight.

Duffy had more sense than to wish for everything at once. When the squire returned from hunting that evening with two fine hares, he sat down before the fire. There were not only steaming meat pies waiting for him—there was as fine a pair of long socks as ever was made.

. . .

As the months passed, the squire became more and more pleased with his housekeeper. The yarn she produced was of the finest quality; the squire's new vests and britches were as strong as could be. And his long socks! The squire never tired of telling his neighbors of the fine socks Duffy produced for him.

"I've worn these socks for almost a year now," he crowed, "and they're as good as new. Duffy's yarn is as strong as leather."

Duffy kept the devil busily at work, and was as pleased as could be with her bargain. She had plenty of time to trot off to the gristmill in the afternoons. There she gossiped cheerfully with the other women of the village as they waited for their grain to be ground. They had a merry time of it, telling old tales and dancing a round or two on the green grass beside the mill.

One evening when the squire came home from his hunting, who should he find in the chimney corner but Huey the widower, who had come a-courting.

The squire frowned and scowled until finally Huey took himself off.

The next night, Jock, the miller's son, was in the chimney corner.

"What's *he* after?" growled the squire when Jock had left.

"I suppose he's come a-courting and to sample my meat pies," said Duffy.

Almost every evening there was someone sitting in the chimney corner, and it didn't take the squire very long to figure out that the widowers and bachelors of the village all had their eye on Duffy.

"I'll lose my treasure!" he thought in panic. There was only one thing to be done.

"Duffy," said the squire, "would you like to be a squire's wife?"

"I would indeed," said Duffy.

"Then we'd best get married," said he.

Duffy was now the squire's lady, but little else was changed. Aside from wearing finer clothes, she was the same cheerful Duffy, dancing and gossiping with the village women at the mill. She produced the same strong yarn and well-knit clothes. Each evening, when the squire returned from hunting, he found a tasty dinner and an orderly house.

But the three years were running out.

The sharp-faced little man started turning up among the wool sacks, or on top of the kitchen woodpile, jeering, "Only a month more, Duffy my dear, and away you go with me!"

Duffy scowled at him. She had tried every means she knew to find out the gloating devil's name. Not a clue could she find.

"Only two weeks more, Duffy," he said, grinning as he flicked his long tail. "You'll never never guess my name!" She threw a pot at him, but he vanished immediately and the pot crashed against the wall.

She went off at once to consult her friend, Old Bet, at the mill.

"I know a thing or two about devils and imps," said Old Bet. "I'll see what we can do."

"Only one more week, Duffy my girl," crowed the sharp-faced little man, popping up beside her in the kitchen. She took a swing at him, but he was gone in an instant and her fist hit the table with a thump.

Rubbing her sore knuckles, she hurried down to Old Bet. "He'll drive me daft with his jeering and his threats," cried Duffy. "I'm that worried! We'll never learn his name!"

But Bet had a plan. "Take a jug of the strongest and best applejack from the squire's cellar and bring it to me at sundown," said Bet.

At sundown the squire was still out hunting. Duffy picked out a large jug of the best jack and carried it down to the green beside the mill.

"Tonight's a full moon," said Bet. "The devils and the witches are gathering to dance at the Devil's Basin out on the moor, and I shall thump the tambourine for them. Come along now before they arrive."

Wrapping herself in a red cloak, and picking up the jug and tambourine, Old Bet hurried off with Duffy trotting behind her. When they arrived at the Devil's Basin, a hollow in the moors, it was almost dark.

"Hide yourself well in these furze bushes," ordered Bet, "and whatever happens, do not make a sound."

So Duffy crouched down in the scratchy furze bushes to wait, with barely a peephole through the branches to peer through.

Soon she heard a great rustling and chattering, and she wondered how many witches had flown in to the meeting place. Through her peephole in the bushes she saw a fire lit. It burned with a high blue flame.

Old Bet was seated near the fire, the jug of applejack in front of her. She thumped her tambourine and the dancing began.

Round and round the fire went the dancers—and the little devil with the long tail danced with them. Every time he came round, he'd pause to take a deep swig from the jug, until finally he became as loud and merry as a grig.

Roaring with drunken laughter he jumped up and down, twirling his tail and singing:

"Duffy my lady, you'll never guess that
My name is Terrytop, Terrytop, Terrytop!"

At that moment the baying of hounds after hare filled the air. Across the moor in the moonlight rode the squire with his hounds, heading straight for the Devil's Basin.

With a screech and a whoop, the dancers vanished. The tambourine ceased, and the fire died out.

Duffy scrambled out of the furze bushes and ran like the wind for home. She barely had time to stir the stew and settle down panting beside the fire when the squire came in.

"What a bad time of it I had this day!" he cried. "Not a hare did the hounds raise till after sundown. And a funny thing happened, Duffy. We chased that hare all over the moor by moonlight until we headed straight for a pack of witches dancing round a fire! What do you think of that, Duffy?"

Duffy shook her head in wonder. "It's bad luck, you know, to break in on witches dancing. What did they do?"

"They up and disappeared in a flash. Nothing left that I could see but an empty jug lying on the moor. Nay, I didn't go close to the place, for I feared the witches' curse." He sighed heavily. "I never did get the hare."

. . .

The three years of Duffy's bargain were up. On the appointed day, the sharp-faced little devil appeared in Duffy's kitchen.

"Your time's up, Duffy my dear," said he, smirking and flicking his tail. "I've kept my part of the bargain, now off you go with me."

"Not so fast, sir," said Duffy. "There was more to the bargain than that."

"Ha! You think you can guess my name?" He grinned. "I'll give you three guesses."

"Maybe it is Lucifer?" asked Duffy.

The devil sputtered with laughter and thumped his tail on the floor. "An acquaintance of mine," he said at last.

"Perhaps it is Beelzebub?"

"A cousin of mine, but a low, common sort," he said in disdain. "Come along now. You'll never guess my name—it's not generally known on earth." And he made as if to lay hands on her.

"Oh, no you don't!" cried Duffy as she dodged out of reach. "Are you honest enough to admit your name is Terrytop?"

The devil stood glaring at her in rage.

"Do you deny your name is Terrytop?" she taunted.

"A gentleman never denies his name," he spat, "but I never expected to be beaten by a minx like you!" And with a puff of smoke he disappeared, never to return.

A moment later, everything in the house that the devil had spun or knitted turned to dust.

When this happened the squire was far away on the moors, hunting as usual. It was a cold day with a piercing wind. Suddenly his long socks dropped off, then his britches, and then every garment that was homespun, till he was clad in nothing at all but his leather shoes and jerkin.

He arrived home blue with cold and shivering like a leaf.

"Ah, Duffy," he said when his teeth stopped chattering and he could speak. "You see what's happened to me! It must be the witches' curse on me for breaking up their dance! Bring me some stockings and britches quickly."

Duffy shook her head sadly. "All the yarn goods in the house must be cursed as well, for they have all turned to dust!"

When the squire saw that this was true, he groaned at his loss. "But you can spin me some more, Duffy!"

Duffy shook her head again. "It will do no good. You can see that all the spinning and knitting done in this house is cursed. We'd best have the work done elsewhere."

This advice didn't please the squire at all, until Duffy said sensibly, "Would you want all your clothes to drop off out on the moors in the dead of winter—or the blankets on our bed to turn to dust on a cold winter's night?"

The very thought of these disasters was enough to convince the squire. "I'd be a laughingstock in the county, if I didn't freeze to death first!" he muttered.

So the squire's spinning and knitting were done in the village. Duffy was well content with her bargain, and the squire hunted happily ever after.

. . .

*L*ong ago, long before the white people came, Canada turned very cold. In all the land there was not a flower nor a tree left alive. Snow and ice were everywhere.

This terrible cold covered the land for a long time. Because the ground was frozen, the Indians could not grow corn. The people were starving, and it seemed as if the whole land must perish.

Although Glooskap, the ruler of the Indian people, was wise and strong, he had no power against the ice and snow covering his land. He tried all his magic, but it was of no use, for this terrible cold was caused by a powerful giant who came into the land from the Far North. His breath could wither trees; he could destroy the corn and kill man and beast.

The giant's name was Winter. He was very old and very strong, and he had ruled in the Far North long before the coming of man.

Glooskap went alone to the giant's ice tent, thinking to bribe or force the Winter Giant to go away. But even Glooskap, with all his magic power, fell under the spell of the beauty of the giant's land. In the sunlight it sparkled like crystal with pinpoints of many colors. The trees, laden with snow, had strange, fantastic shapes. At night the sky was filled with flashing, quivering lights, and even the stars had a rare brilliance.

The giant told tales of ancient times when all the land was silent, white, and beautiful. Then he used his charm of slumber until Glooskap fell asleep. But Glooskap was very strong, and Winter could not kill him, even in his sleep. After he had slept for a long time, Glooskap awoke, rose, and went back to his people.

One day soon after this, his tale-bearer, Tatler the Loon, brought him good news. Far away there was a wonderful Southland where it was always warm. Ruling over this land was a queen who could easily overcome the giant—indeed, she was the only one on earth whose power the giant feared. Glooskap knew the queen could save his people. He decided he must go to the Southland to find her.

She lived, said Tatler the Loon, in the Wilderness of Flowers. And he gave Glooskap directions to find her. Glooskap traveled many miles across the land to the sea. On the shore he sang the magic song that whales obey. His old friend Blob the Whale came quickly to his call. Climbing on to her back, he sailed away.

Now, Blob the Whale had a strange rule for passengers. She said to Glooskap, "You must close your eyes tightly while I carry you. If you open them, I will go aground on a reef or sandbar and be stuck fast. Then you may be drowned." Glooskap promised to keep his eyes tightly closed.

The whale swam for many days. Each day the water grew warmer and the air grew milder. Then the soft air no longer smelled of the salt sea, but of fruit and flowers. They had left the deep sea, and were in the shallow water closer to land.

Blob the Whale now swam more cautiously. Down in the sand the clams were singing a song of warning, telling of the sandbar beneath the water. But the whale did not understand the language of the clams. Glooskap did.

Glooskap thought it would be a good idea if the whale *did* go aground near shore. Then he could more easily walk to land. So he opened his left eye. At once the whale struck a sandbar close to the beach; Glooskap was able to leap from her head and wade ashore.

Stuck fast and fearful that she would never get free, the whale became very angry. But Glooskap put one end of his strong bow against the whale's jaw, and with a mighty push, he sent old Blob back into the deep water.

Walking far inland with great strides, Glooskap soon found the road Loon had described. It was the Rainbow Road, which led to the Wilderness of Flowers. Here the Winter Giant had no power. The winds were always warm; snow and ice were unknown.

Glooskap went quickly along the road until he came to an orange grove where the air was fragrant with blossoms. Not far ahead he saw a clearing, and from it came the sound of singing.

Creeping closer, he stood behind a tree to watch. Around the soft grass of the clearing, every kind of flower was in bloom. Birds with brightly colored feathers fluttered and sang in the trees. He had found old Tatler the Loon's Wilderness of Flowers.

In the open space, four maidens sang a song of summer as they moved through the graceful steps of a dance. Taller and more splendid than the others was a maiden whose long brown hair was crowned with flowers. For some time Glooskap gazed in silence.

Then he noticed nearby an old woman, faded but still beautiful, also watching the dancers.

"Who are these maidens?" he asked

"The maiden with the headdress of flowers is the queen," she answered. "Her name is Summer. The maidens with her are her children: Sunshine, Light, and Flowers."

Here at last was the queen who could challenge Winter and force him to go away! Glooskap began to sing his magic songs, until he lured the Summer Queen to his side.

He spoke to her of his people cold and hungry, of his Northland frozen and desolate under the power of Winter. "Only you can defeat the Winter Giant and save my people," he said.

The Summer Queen considered Glooskap's words. "I will come with you to save your people," she said at last. "But I cannot stay. I must return again to my Southland."

Glooskap nodded. Then, with their hands clasped together, they began the long return journey by land. He ran north with the Summer Queen for many, many days until at last they reached the Northland.

Glooskap was saddened to see his country still desolate and covered with ice. Only a few of his people remained alive—and they had fallen asleep under the Winter Giant's power.

The Summer Queen and Glooskap hurried on to the ice home of Winter. The giant welcomed them with a grin, thinking to freeze both Glooskap and the glowing queen with his power.

How splendidly she stood smiling before the giant! Winter used all his most powerful charms to numb the pair, but the queen softly sang a summer song. The charms of Winter failed.

Large drops ran down the giant's face. His ice tent slowly melted away. The Summer Queen spread her strange power until everything the Winter Giant had frozen came to life. Melted snow ran down the rivers; buds swelled again on trees; grass and corn sprang up with new life.

Angrily the Winter Giant wept with tears like cold rain, for he knew he was defeated.

The Summer Queen spoke: "I have proved that I am more powerful than you, Giant of Winter, but I have no wish to destroy you. I give you all the country of the Far North for your own. You may come back to Glooskap's country every year for six months only; but when you do return here, your stay must be much less severe. When you leave in the spring, I will come from the Southland and rule in Glooskap's country for six months."

Winter bowed his head and accepted the terms—for he feared that if he did not, he would melt away entirely.

And Glooskap was pleased with the queen's generosity, for he did not wish the beauty of snow on the land to be lost forever.

The Winter Giant left at once for the Far North. There he reigns with all his power. In late autumn, when the Summer Queen returns to her homeland, the Winter Giant comes back to Glooskap's country. But at the end of six months, the Summer Queen always returns with songbirds and bright flowers to drive the Winter Giant back to his northern home.

In this way, the fair Summer Queen and the ancient Winter Giant divide the land of Canada between them.

THE STARS IN THE SKY

An English Tale

• • •

*T*here once was a girl who wanted to touch the stars in the sky.

On clear nights, when she looked through her bedroom window, the stars twinkled and glittered in the velvet blackness of the sky above. Sometimes the stars seemed like diamonds, sometimes like tears, and sometimes like merry eyes.

One summer evening the lass set off to seek the stars. She walked and walked until she came to the dark, satiny surface of a millpond.

"Good evening," said she. "I'm seeking the stars in the sky. Can you help me?"

"They're right here," murmured the pond. "They shine so brightly on my face that I can't sleep nights. Jump in, lass. See if you can catch one."

The lass jumped into the pond and swam all around it. But never a star did she find.

She walked on across the fields until she came to a chattering brook.

"Good evening," said she. "I'm off to find the stars in the sky. Do you know how to reach them?"

"Yes, yes. They're always dancing about on the stones and water here," chattered the brook. "Come in and catch one if you can."

The lass waded in, but not a star could she find in the brook.

"I don't think the stars come down here at all!" she cried.

"Well, they *look* as if they're here," said the brook pertly. "And isn't that the same thing?"

"Not the same thing at all," said the girl.

She walked on until she met a host of Little Folk dancing on the grass. No taller than herself, they seemed very elegant in their clothes of green and gold.

"Good evening to you, Little Folk of the Hill," she called, taking care to be polite. "I'm seeking the stars in the sky."

High, silvery voices rang out. "They shine on the grass here at night. Come dance with us if you want to find one."

The lass joined the round ring dance of the Little Folk and danced and danced. But although the grass twinkled and gleamed beneath their feet, not a star did she find.

She left the dancers and sat down beyond the ring. "I've searched and searched, but there are no stars down here," she cried. "Can't you tell me how to reach the stars?"

The dancers simply laughed. Then one of the company came over to her and said, "Since you're so set on it, I'll give you this advice. If you won't go back, go forward. Keep going forward; and mind you take the right road. Ask Four-Feet to carry you to No-Feet-At-All. Then tell No-Feet-At-All to carry you to the Stairs Without Steps. If you can climb them—"

"If I can, will I be up among the stars in the sky at last?" she asked.

"If you're not there, you'll be somewhere else," said the Little Man, and he ran back to join the dancers.

With a light heart, the lass stood up and went forward. Just as she was beginning to doubt that she was on the right road, she came to a silver-gray horse beneath a rowan tree.

"Good evening," said the lass. "I'm seeking the stars in the sky and my feet are weary. Will you carry me along the way?"

"I know nothing about stars in the sky," said the horse. "I am here to do the bidding of the Little Folk only."

"I've just been dancing with them, and I was told to ask Four-Feet to carry me to No-Feet-At-All."

"In that case, climb on my back," said the horse. "I am Four-Feet, and I will take you there."

They rode on and on until they left the woods behind and came to the edge of the land. Before them on the water, a wide, gleaming path of silver ran straight out to sea. And in the distance, a wonderful arch of brilliant colors rose from the water and went right up into the sky.

"I've brought you to the end of land," said the horse. "That's as much as Four-Feet can do for you. Climb down now; I must be off."

The lass slid from the horse and stood on the shore, looking about her. A large fish swam in from the sea.

"Good evening, fish," she called. "I'm looking for the stars in the sky. Can you show me the way?"

"Not unless you bring the word of the Little Folk," said the fish.

"I can indeed," she answered. "Four-Feet brought me here, and I was told No-Feet-At-All would carry me to the Stairs Without Steps."

"In that case," said the fish, "I will take you. Sit on my back and hold tight."

Off he swam with the girl on his back, straight along the silver path toward the bright arch of many colors. As they came to the foot of it, she saw the broad stairs of color rising steeply into the sky. At the far end of it were the merry, glittering stars.

"Here you are," said the fish. "These are the Stairs Without Steps. They're not easy to climb. Climb if you can, but mind you hold fast and don't fall!"

So she started off. It was not easy at all to climb the bright-colored light. She climbed on and on, and it seemed she moved very slowly. Although she was high above the sea, the stars were still far away.

She was very weary but she thought, "I've come this far. I won't give up now."

On and on she went. The air grew colder, the light more brilliant, until at last she reached the top of the arch. All about her the stars darted, raced, and spun in dazzling flashes of light. Below her, stretching down into darkness, were the brilliant colors of the Stairs Without Steps.

She had reached the stars in the sky at last, and she stood transfixed with joy at the sheer wonder of it all.

After a time she became aware that the air was icy cold, and the hard, brilliant light of the spinning stars made her dizzy. Shading her eyes with her hand, she tried to see the earth below, but all was in darkness. No warm flicker of hearth or candlelight could be seen.

Then, in one last yearning effort, she stretched out her hand to touch a flashing star. She reached farther, farther—until suddenly she lost her balance. With a sigh—half of regret, half of contentment—she slid down, down, faster and faster into the darkness below, and all sense left her.

When she opened her eyes it was morning. The sun shone warm and golden on her bed.

"I *did* reach the stars!" she thought with joy. But in the safe stillness of her room she wondered, "Or did I dream it?"

Then she opened her tightly curled right hand, and on her palm lay a brilliant speck of stardust.

LANVAL AND THE LADY TRIAMOR

A Breton / Celtic Tale

• • •

A very long time ago there lived a young noble-
man named Lanval, whose only ambition was to be a champion. In
all the principal castles of the country, knights competed in jousts
and tilting bouts; Lanval longed to win fame as the greatest champion of all.

When Lanval was scarcely eighteen years of age, he came into a
comfortable inheritance, and he set off at once for the castle of the
nearest earl. He bought the finest horses and armor, the richest
clothes. He was openhanded and generous to everyone. In short, he
lived as if there could be no end to his wealth.

Lanval stood well in the earl's favor and was popular with the
knights who thronged the earl's castle. He had only one fault: he
often spoke impulsively, without thought.

One day the earl announced that he was going to marry King Ryan's daughter, from Ireland. This choice privately dismayed his knights and companions.

"King Ryan's daughter!" exclaimed Lanval impulsively. "I'm sorry to hear that!"

"Are you indeed? What do you have against the lady?" asked the earl.

Lanval now felt uncomfortable and wished he could learn to hold his tongue. Everyone at the castle had gossiped about the lady. Few thought her a wise choice for a bride—but no one had spoken this aloud to the earl.

"It's said she's mean and sharp-tempered," answered Lanval lamely.

"The lady brings a good dowry and is the most beautiful of Ryan's daughters," said the earl coldly. "That is enough for me."

So, with many days of feasting, the marriage took place. But ill-said words travel fast, and the lady took a dislike to Lanval. On the last day of the wedding feast, the new countess gave a lavish gift to each of the earl's knights—except Lanval. This pointed public insult was more than Lanval could bear. He felt his days as companion to the earl were over; there was nothing to do but withdraw from the castle.

Taking a small band of retainers with him, he rode off aimlessly, staying at one castle after another, jousting in every tournament. And of course he spent money as freely as ever.

Barely a year later he found himself penniless. His retainers, long unpaid, rode away. Unable to pay his bill, Lanval stayed on at the inn where he had lodged. His fine tournament steeds and gear were gone; he had not even money for food. He was in the lowest depths of despair. He could not think what to do.

Borrowing a hack horse for a few hours from the innkeeper's kindhearted daughter, he rode out from the town and into the forest. Here he dismounted and sat down to consider his bleak future.

It was at this point that the lady Triamor decided to take a hand in Lanval's fortunes. Lanval's youth and ambition had taken her fancy—and women of the fairy world are known to admire openhanded generosity in humans.

Lanval was quite startled to see the lady Triamor appear suddenly before him. She had all the unearthly radiance and dazzling beauty that fairy women can assume at will. Her garments were of shimmering green, adorned with precious jewels, and her red-gold hair lay like glowing silk over her shoulders. Lanval was enchanted in every sense of the word.

When the lady Triamor began to speak, it was clear at once that she knew his situation.

"What a pity that a brave and generous knight should be brought so low!" she said. "I would like to help you, dear Lanval."

"I am—grateful," stammered Lanval.

"I can give you what you most desire: a purse full of gold that will never be empty. No matter how many coins you take out, it will always be full. I can give you Blanchard, the finest tournament horse in the world, together with my banner and Gifre, my groom. As long as you carry my banner as you ride, you will win every joust and every combat you undertake. No blow can harm you."

Lanval, stunned with joy, was scarcely able to believe his good fortune.

"However, there are certain conditions attached to these gifts. You must forsake all other women and pledge yourself only to me. Although I will be invisible to others, I will come to you whenever and wherever you call me, to be your love. *But remember this:* If you ever speak to any human about me, our pact ends at once."

"Your conditions are easy. I gladly agree to them," said he. "I am already deeply in love with you."

Lanval returned to the inn on the splendid white charger, Blanchard, attended by the groom, Gifre, riding the hack. In Lanval's saddlebag was a heavy bag of gold.

The lady Triamor's favor brought Lanval all that he had longed for. He won fame as champion in every jousting tournament in the land. In addition, his wealth was unending, and the radiant Triamor came to his chamber whenever he wished.

After several years of traveling about, he returned to visit the castle of his former patron and friend, the earl.

The earl's countess noticed that Lanval, though wealthy, was still unmarried; although he was courteous to all the young ladies of the court, he favored none of them.

Seeking him out when he was alone, the countess said to him spitefully, "None of the fine ladies here seem to please you. I think it very strange that after all these years you love no woman, and no woman loves you!"

Alas, Lanval still had not learned to hold his tongue.

"That's not true," he retorted. "I have my own lady, far more enchanting than anyone here!"

"I doubt that!" sneered the countess, for she was extremely vain about her looks. "Although you've won fame and fortune, no one has seen this lady you speak of. Do you hide her away because she is so ugly and ill-favored?"

"My lady Triamor is the most beautiful woman in the world!" cried Lanval angrily. "Next to her, all the ladies in this castle are plain and dowdy!"

This insult was of course unforgivable, and the countess rushed at once to the earl.

Lanval returned to his chamber, ashamed of his thoughtless temper. There he found that his bag of gold was empty. When he looked out the window, he saw Gifre, holding Triamor's banner, trotting away from the castle on Blanchard.

The full weight of the disaster struck him like a blow. All was lost, including his lady Triamor. He was penniless again.

It was not long before fresh disaster overwhelmed Lanval. He was summoned to the earl's presence to answer charges before the assembled court.

The countess charged that Lanval had asked to be her lover and that when she had angrily repulsed him, he had said she and all the ladies of the castle were plain and dowdy. Both insults were intolerable. The countess demanded Lanval's death.

Needless to say, the earl was furious at this abuse of his friendship and hospitality. He listened to Lanval's explanation, but he did not believe him.

"I swear I did nothing—said nothing of love to the countess!" Lanval pleaded. "I said my lady Triamor was so enchantingly beautiful she would make the ladies of the castle seem plain. I apologize to the ladies for my discourteous words. But I spoke only the truth about my lady Triamor!"

Many of those assembled in the great hall for the trial were friends of Lanval. They knew him to be thoughtless and impulsive—but also generous and honest. In addition, they knew the mean temper of the countess.

"If the knight Lanval spoke only the truth about his own lady, surely he should not be punished by death!" they cried.

At last the earl was persuaded that this was fair. Lanval must produce his lady Triamor, and if all agreed she was as radiant in beauty as Lanval claimed, he would be pardoned.

Sadly, Lanval returned to his chamber. He tried again and again to summon Triamor, but she did not appear. Their pact was broken.

The earl had given Lanval seven weeks to produce his lady. As the time passed, Lanval's friends eyed him anxiously. The countess wore an air of smug triumph. And all Lanval could do was to ride hopelessly through all the forests in the earl's domain, searching for Triamor.

When the seven weeks had passed, the earl and the court assembled in the great hall to pass judgment on Lanval.

"I cannot bring my lady Triamor before this court," confessed Lanval. "I love her dearly, but I broke my word to her, and she has forsaken me."

A deep sigh of sorrow rippled through the company. Lanval was doomed.

Just then a cry rang out: "Look! Someone comes!"

Through the great open archway of the entrance they could see a party of riders coming toward the castle. A buzz of speculation rose from the company.

Over the drawbridge the lady Triamor rode with seven attendants, all clad in jeweled cloth of gold. Each maiden was lovely, but the golden radiance of the lady Triamor stunned and dazzled all who gazed at her.

"Is this your lady?" asked the earl when he could find his voice.

"This is my lady Triamor." Lanval went to her and knelt down for forgiveness.

And so powerful are the enchantments of fairy women that all the company in the hall stood transfixed. Not one could deny that Triamor was more dazzling than any woman in the world.

"The knight Lanval is freed of the charge against him," said the earl.

Triamor motioned for Lanval to leap up behind her on her horse. When he was seated, the party turned and rode out of the castle. As long as they were in sight, no one could move or speak a word.

Where they went nobody knows, for young Lanval was never seen again in this world.

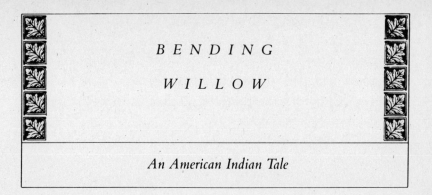

BENDING
WILLOW

An American Indian Tale

• • •

Long ago, the young Indian maiden Bending Willow lived in the wigwam of her parents, not far from the great falls called Niagará. The tribe was at peace, the waterfowl and fish from the river were plentiful. But Bending Willow was very unhappy.

Although several young warriors sought her in marriage, the most persistent and most unwelcome suitor was the chief, a cruel old man rightly named No Heart. His hair was as gray as a badger and he had already buried three wives. However, he had great power in the tribe, and when he declared that he would take Bending Willow for his next wife, her parents dared not refuse him.

Bending Willow had another reason for sadness; she had no

living brother or sister to help or advise her. They had died from the mysterious sickness that so often attacked members of the tribe. Since her close friend, Laughing Water, had been taken, Bending Willow felt very much alone.

The tribe blamed an evil spirit loose in the village for the mysterious sickness. Chief No Heart proclaimed that the marriage celebration of a chief would drive away this evil spirit. Then he set the day for the ceremony.

When Bending Willow was told of this, she ran into the forest to be alone and think. She would not marry Chief No Heart. She did not believe the mysterious sickness would disappear if the marriage took place. At last she could think of only one solution: she must leave the village and escape to the lands across the wide river.

Early the next morning before dawn, when all were sleeping, she dragged her father's canoe to the edge of the river, stepped into it, and paddled swiftly out into the current.

The night was still dark, with very few stars gleaming in the blackness above her, and the current at this time of the year was much stronger than she had expected. She paddled with all her strength for some time without success. Instead of making her way across the wide river, she found herself at dawn headed toward the rapids.

The paddle was torn from her hands as the canoe tossed about wildly, like a withered branch, on the white-crested waves. The roar of the great falls filled her ears. Swiftly but surely she was borne toward the rocks at the edge of the great falls.

She raised her eyes to the distant star still gleaming steadily in the morning grayness above. If only the Star Maiden would lift her up to the heavens!

"I would rather be up in the sky forever than down at the bottom of the river!" she thought.

For one moment only she saw the bright white and green foam

of water. Then she felt herself lifted on great white wings above the rocks. The water divided, and she passed into a dark cave behind the foaming spray.

In the cave was a small creature with a white face and hair of soft white mist, like the mist that rises from the base of the falls. It was the water spirit, Cloud-and-Rain, who had rescued her and taken her into his lodge. The door of his lodge was the green wave of Niagara, and the walls of the cave were of gray rock studded with white stone flowers.

Cloud-and-Rain gave her a warm wrapper and seated her on a heap of ermine skins in a far corner where the dampness was shut out by a magic fire. He brought her fish to eat and delicate jelly made from mosses only the water spirits can find.

When she was rested, Cloud-and-Rain told her he knew her story. "No Heart is not a wise leader for your people," he said. "The campsite of the village is a bad one. It is too close to the swamp. When the sickness came, he did not listen to the elders' advice to move."

"You know of the mysterious sickness!" cried Bending Willow. "It has taken my brothers and sister and my friend Laughing Water. No one knows what evil spirit brings it or how to drive it away!"

"There are herbs to help and knowledge of how to use them. That I can teach you." Cloud-and-Rain was silent for a time. "Yes, there are many things I can teach you that will help your people. The water of your village is bad, poisoned."

"Poisoned?" Bending Willow stared at him in perplexity. "What evil spirit did that? I do not understand."

"Listen carefully if you would save the lives of your tribe," said the water spirit Cloud-and-Rain. "A great serpent lies underneath the ground of your village. He poisons the springs from which you draw the water to drink. When people die, the serpent is pleased, and more and more poison seeps into your springs. Even now the spring that No Heart uses is fouled, and he will soon die."

"If you can teach me how the village can get rid of this evil serpent, I will stay with you gladly," said Bending Willow.

"When you return," said Cloud-and-Rain, "you must persuade your people to move their camp. Let them come to dwell nearer to me, in the high upland."

Bending Willow stayed three months with Cloud-and-Rain. He taught her much medicine skill, and showed her the herbs to cure sickness.

One day when he came in from fishing, he said to her, "Chief No Heart is dead. This night I will throw a bridge from the foot of the waters across the falls to the high hills. You must climb it without fear, for I will hold it firmly until you are on the land."

When the moon rose, casting a gleam of silver on the waters, Cloud-and-Rain caused a gentle wind to raise the spray until it formed a great white arch reaching from his cave to the distant hills. He led Bending Willow to the foot of this bridge of mist and helped her start off. Higher and higher she climbed, brave and confident, until she descended the misty arch onto the high upland.

When she returned to the village, the tribe welcomed her joyfully. No one blamed her for leaving the tribe to escape marriage with No Heart. They listened quietly when she told them of the water spirit Cloud-and-Rain, and of the medicine wisdom he had taught her. But they would not agree to move their village to the uplands.

"The swamp is a protection against enemy attack," they said. "And there are plentiful fish and waterfowl here."

"The upland farther down the river is safer," she answered. "The water is pure. There are many herbs and plants to cure sickness. Here the water springs are poisoned by an evil serpent spirit who lies hidden under the ground." But they shook their heads in disbelief.

When the tribe would not accept the wisdom she had brought from the water spirit, Bending Willow at first felt discouraged. But the months she had spent with Cloud-and-Rain had given her confidence and courage, as well as wisdom. She spoke to her mother and other women of the village separately. Several of them were persuaded that the water spirit's advice was sound.

Bending Willow led these women to the high uplands to draw their water from the clear springs bubbling out from the rocks. Then the women carried the water carefully back to the village. They did this for several months. Neither the women nor any of their families who used this water fell ill. Of those using the village water, some sickened—and among them were strong warriors as well as two of the new chief's children.

This was enough to convince the new chief. The tribe held a council and voted to move. They took down their lodgepoles and moved the village to the uplands.

There the tribe lived in peace and good health. Bending Willow shared her knowledge of herbs with the women of the tribe. And before many months had passed, she happily married a young warrior of her choice.

FINN MAGIC

A Scandinavian Tale

· · ·

Far to the north, on the bleak coast of the Northern Seas, there once lived a lad named Eilert. His family were fisher folk, and they lived beside a rocky headland jutting out into the sea. Their nearest neighbors, who lived some distance along the shore on the other side of the cliff, were a family of Finns.

Both Eilert's family and the Finns used the same fishing grounds, but there was no friendliness between them. Eilert's family were Nordlanders, and they were sure the Finns used their special magic against them.

Eilert's father muttered angrily, "Heathen charms and spells!" when the Finns hauled in a good catch and his own was small.

The Nordlanders along that coast thought the Finns were strange folk with a knowledge of ancient magic. The Finns had black hair, wore odd clothes, and talked among themselves in a peculiar language. All their habits and customs were strange, and their burial ground in the village was separate and apart from the Nordlanders' graves.

Eilert did not share his father's fear of the Finns' magic. When he was a small child playing on the rocky headland, he had met Zilla, a Finn girl his own age. They had become friends, and he had often gone home with her to the Finns' place on the other side of the headland. Zilla was thin and wiry, but she was strong. She could run like a hare and handle a boat as well as he could.

The Finns were kind to him. He saw no evil in them. Nonetheless he thought it best not to tell his family where he had been whenever he returned from a visit to Zilla's place.

Nor did he tell his family of the strange tales the Finns told of Mermen and Draugs who dragged fishermen under the waves to their homes at the bottom of the sea. The Mermen had heads like seals; the Draugs were evil creatures with heads of seaweed.

Eilert and the Nordlanders knew of course that Mermen lived under the Northern Seas, waiting for victims. But the Finns seemed to have an uncanny knowledge of this kingdom beneath the sea, and claimed that their ancestors had often visited there.

Walking home across the headland after hearing these tales, Eilert shivered and wondered if the Finns did indeed have a strange power over the sea. But the lass Zilla was friendly and merry, and the Finns seemed to be kind, cheerful folk, so he put the thought away from him.

Now it happened that one autumn Eilert's family was having a very lean time of it. Day after day on the fishing grounds his father's lines caught next to nothing, while not far off, a dark-haired Finn pulled up one fine catch after another. Eilert's father swore the Finn was making strange signs in the air and using magic spells against him.

"I'd use our counter-charm," cried his father angrily, "but I don't dare. It's said the Merfolk take a terrible revenge on those who do!"

Eilert became very troubled. Was the Finn using magic to lure all the fish to his lines? He felt guilty about his secret friendship with Zilla and the Finns—could this be the cause of his father's bad luck?

He stopped his visits to the Finns' place, and he no longer walked with Zilla under the pines on the headland. But this did not help at all. Day after day, Eilert's father set out his lines and drew them in almost empty of fish.

Eilert knew the counter-charm was dangerous, for it put the user in the power of the Merfolk. But he made up his mind that he himself must use it. He must take earth from the grave of a Finn and rub it on his father's fishing line.

Late the next night he went off secretly to the Finn graveyard and put a handful of earth from a Finn grave into his pocket. When he returned home he rubbed the earth on all his father's fishing lines.

The very next day his father hauled in a fine catch, and this good luck continued day after day. The counter-charm had worked. But each day Eilert's fear of the Draugs and Merfolk increased. To avoid their revenge, he went back to the Finn grave one night to beg forgiveness. But he also took care to carry a piece of iron in his pocket at all times, as protection against sorcery.

One day Eilert went out alone to fish for Greenland shark, for the fish brought a fine price at market. As he rowed, he did not look in the direction of the Finns' place, nor did he notice the lass Zilla watching him from the shore. He rowed on out of sight.

When a shark at last took his line, it was a huge one. Although the boat was small, Eliert would not give up his efforts to pull the shark alongside. At last the shark tore off with Eilert's line taut behind him. Then, unable to lose the fishing line, the shark twisted and plunged suddenly down to the depths of the sea. The boat capsized.

Faint and numb with cold, Eilert clung to the hull of the over-turned boat as it tossed in the rough sea. Suddenly he saw, sitting on one end of the boat, a large creature with a seaweed head and a neck like a seal. The two reddish eyes glared at him. The Draug slowly forced its end of the boat down under the water.

"You rubbed your lines with grave earth," hissed the Draug. "Now the people of the sea seek their revenge."

Eilert closed his eyes in despair. He felt himself sinking down under the waves. When he opened his eyes, the frightening Draug was gone, but he saw that he was standing on the bottom of the sea near his overturned boat.

The floor of the sea was of white sand, and the light around him was pale gray, but strangely he did not feel cold or wet. Then he saw a Mermaid beside him.

"I have rescued you from the Draug," she said. "Come, now I must take you to my father, the king of the Merfolk."

The Mermaid's black seaweed hair floated out from her head; her face was pale, with dark, gleaming eyes. Her form was clad in a greenish substance, and the silver brooch she wore had the same strange design the Finns used.

Eilert walked with the Mermaid along the sandy bottom. On either side were meadows of sea grass and bushes of thick seaweed. They passed brightly colored shells and broken hulls of boats half buried in the sand.

At last they came to a house made from the hulls of two ships. The Mermaid led Eilert through the door, which she closed behind him. Inside, seated on a rough chair, was a large Merman. His head and neck were like a seal's, but his face resembled that of a dogfish. The fingers on both hands were webbed together, his feet covered in old sea boots.

"Well, Eilert," said the Merman, grinning, "you've had a very bad time of it up there today. Sit down, sit down."

Eilert saw nowhere to sit but on a pile of old nets. When he was seated, the old Merman shook his head sadly. "You should not have taken our grave earth to rub on your lines. But you're here now, so you might as well make the best of it."

Eilert could think of nothing to say; he put his hand into his pocket to touch the piece of iron. The Merman brought out a jug of strong Northern brandy.

"Drink up! Drink up!" he cried, pouring the brandy into cups.

Eilert drank one cup, then another. He decided he had had enough. But the Merman drank merrily on, finishing one jug after another while the dark-haired Mermaid stood silently at the door.

At last the Merman sighed and leaned back with glazed eyes. Without a sound, he slid slowly to the floor and slept.

"Come," said the Mermaid. "He will sleep like that for hours."

He followed her back along the sea floor until they reached his boat where it lay on the sand.

The Mermaid turned to him. "If I am to help you escape and return to the world above, you must lie down in the boat now and sleep."

Eilert hesitated, but the Mermaid's eyes were as kind as Zilla's and he was very tired. He lay down in the boat and closed his eyes. He felt her black seaweed hair spread around him like a dark curtain. As he drifted off to sleep, he heard her chanting a strange song.

When Eilert opened his eyes, he looked about in wonder. He was safe in the Finns' house, and Zilla and her father sat close by. Zilla's long black hair lay over her shoulders; her dark eyes stared at him from her pale face.

"I was under the sea with the Merfolk," he cried. "How—how—"

The room was still. Zilla and her father exchanged glances. Then the old man said evasively, "Aye. Our Zilla brought you back. She knows a thing or two about the sea, does Zilla!"

So it was Zilla who had saved him! Eilert wondered what powers she had used. He thought it best not to question; it was enough to know she had rowed out to sea to bring him home.

Now when a lass, Finn or Nordlander, sets about rescuing the lad of her choice—whether by magic or otherwise—there can be only one outcome. The following spring, Zilla and Eilert were married.

It was the first time a Nordlander had married a Finn, and everyone in the village was surprised. But Eilert's parents, on thinking the matter over, had concluded that if the Finns did indeed possess magic spells over fish and other creatures of the sea, it was much better to have them in the family than not.

THE HUSBAND WHO STAYED AT HOME.

A Norwegian Tale

• • •

*O*nce upon a time there was a man so cross and bad-tempered that he thought his wife never did anything right in the house.

So one evening during the haymaking time, when he came home scolding and complaining, his wife said, "You think you could do the work of the house better than I?"

"Yes, I do," growled the husband. "Any man could!"

"Well, then, tomorrow let's switch our tasks. I'll go with the mowers and mow the hay. You stay here and do the housework."

The husband agreed at once. He thought it a very good idea.

Early the next morning his wife took a scythe over her shoulder and went out to the hayfield with the mowers; the man stayed in the house to do the work at home.

He decided first to churn the butter for their dinner. After he had churned awhile, he became thirsty; he went down to the cellar to tap a pitcher of ale. He had just taken the bung out of the ale barrel and was about to put in the tap when overhead he heard the pig come into the kitchen.

With the tap in his hand, he ran up the cellar steps as fast as he could, lest the pig upset the butter churn. When he came up to the kitchen, he saw that the pig had already knocked over the churn. The cream had run all over the floor and the pig was happily slurping it.

He became so wild with rage that he quite forgot the ale barrel in the cellar. He ran after the pig, slipped, and fell facedown into the cream.

When he scrambled to his feet, he caught the pig running through the door and gave it such a kick in the head that the pig dropped dead.

All at once he remembered the ale tap in his hand. But when he ran down to the cellar, every drop of ale had run out of the barrel.

There was still no butter for their dinner, so he went into the dairy to look for more cream. Luckily there was enough cream left to fill the churn once more, and he again began to churn butter.

After he had thumped the churn for a while, he remembered that their milking cow was still shut up in the barn. The poor cow had had nothing to eat or drink all morning, and the sun was now high in the sky.

He had no time to take the cow down to the pasture, for the baby was crawling about in the spilt cream, and he still had to clean up the floor and the baby. He thought it would save time if he put the cow on the top of their house to graze. The flat roof of the house was thatched with sod, and a fine crop of grass was growing there.

Since the house lay close to a steep hill at the back, he thought that if he laid two planks across the thatched roof to the hill, he could easily get the cow up there to graze.

As he started out the door he realized he should not leave the churn in the kitchen with the baby crawling about. "The child is sure to upset it!" he thought.

So he lifted the churn onto his back and went out with it.

"I had best give the cow some water before I put her on the roof to graze," he said to himself. He took up a bucket to draw water from the well, but as he leaned over the well to fill the bucket, all the cream ran out of the churn, over his shoulders, and down into the well.

In a temper, he hurled the empty churn across the yard and went to water the cow. Then he searched for two planks to make a bridge from the hill to the roof of the house. After a great deal of trouble, he persuaded the cow to cross the planks onto the sod roof.

Now it was near dinnertime and the baby was crying. "I have no butter," he thought. "I'd best boil porridge."

So he hurried back to the kitchen, filled the pot with water, and hung it over the fire. Then he realized the cow was not tied; she could easily fall off the roof and break her legs.

Back he ran to the roof with a rope. Since there was no post to tie her to, he tied one end of the rope around the cow, and the other end he slipped down the hole in the roof that served as a chimney. When he came back to the kitchen he tied the loose end around his knee.

The water was now boiling in the pot, but the oatmeal still had to be ground for the porridge. He ground away and was just throwing the oatmeal into the pot when the cow fell off the roof.

As she fell, the rope on the man's knee jerked, and he was pulled up into the air. The pot of water was knocked over, putting the fire out, and the man dangled upside down above the hearth. Outside, the poor cow swung halfway down the house wall, unable to get up or down.

In the meantime, the wife had mowed seven lengths and seven breadths of the hayfield. She expected her husband to call her home to dinner. When he did not appear, she at last trudged off to their home.

When she got there, she saw the cow dangling in such a queer place that she ran up and cut the rope with her scythe. As soon as the rope was cut, the man fell down the hearth.

His wife rushed into the house to find her husband in the hearth, covered with ashes, the floor slippery with clots of cream and ground oatmeal, and the baby wailing.

When they had cleaned up the house and taken the cow out to pasture and hung up the pig for butchering, they sat down to eat stale bread without butter or porridge.

The wife said to him, "Tomorrow you'll get the right way of it."

"Tomorrow!" he sputtered. "You'll not be going out with the mowers tomorrow!"

"And why not? You agreed to it," said she. "Do you think the work of the house too hard?"

This the husband would not admit. "No indeed! If you can do it, I can do it!" he growled.

"Well, then!" said his wife.

They argued the rest of the day over who should mow and who should mind the house. There seemed no way to settle it until at last the husband agreed that he would work in the fields three days a week and work in the house three days; his wife would take his place in the fields for three days, and take care of the house the other days.

With this compromise they lived quite peaceably, and neither the husband nor the wife complained very much at all.

. . .

$\mathbb{A}$ very long time ago, a young woman named Scheherazade lived in the lovely city of Samarkand. It was a city of fragrant gardens, elegant marble fountains, and heavily laden fruit trees. But a dark shadow of fear lay across the city, for a cruel Sultan ruled there.

Scheherazade's father was one of the Sultan's chief advisers. Thus the shadow of fear did not touch her directly, but it lay heavily upon every other family in the city who had a daughter, and Scheherazade shared their grief and terror.

It seemed as though the Sultan had in truth gone mad. Suspecting that the Sultana had been unfaithful, he had had her put to death. Since then, he had demanded that young maidens of the city be brought to him, one after another, as brides. But each "bride" lasted scarcely more than a day or two before she either bored or enraged the Sultan—and she was thrown into a dark dungeon. Many of the daughters in the city had already disappeared, and those who remained lived in terror.

Scheherazade was deeply troubled and turned over in her mind what could be done to stop the Sultan's reign of terror. She was well educated in all areas of history and literature, for her father had provided her with the best tutors in the country. But more to the point, she was clever and courageous as well.

One day she said to her father, "I have a favor to ask of you."

"I can refuse you nothing," said he affectionately.

"I am determined to stop this barbarous behavior of the Sultan. As long as this terrible fate hangs over us, no woman in the city is safe."

"That is true," said her father heavily. "But how can you stop him? Neither the pleas of his advisers nor the heavy grief of the people have any effect."

"Today the Sultan has demanded that a new maiden must be sent to his chambers in the palace. I want you to tell him that I am willing to go," she answered calmly.

"Have you lost your senses?" cried her father in horror. "He is a half-mad old man!"

"Someone must free the women of the city from this evil," she replied. "I have a plan how this may be done."

He shook his head in anguish. "If you do not care about your fate, think of the grief it would cause me. You are the pride of my heart. You have had the finest masters to teach you. With all your cleverness and learning, how can you wish to sacrifice yourself?"

"The Sultan's vicious behavior must be stopped," she repeated. "No woman in the city, or the country, will be safe until it ends. How can I sit here with my books and do nothing?"

Her father continued to plead with her, but she would not change her mind. Sadly he went to the Sultan and said he would bring his daughter Scheherazade to him the next evening.

This news astonished the Sultan. "Is this really your wish?"

"It is not my wish, Your Highness, but my daughter's."

This surprised the Sultan even more.

Early on the appointed day, Scheherazade spoke to her younger sister. "I have a favor to ask of you. Will you come with me when I go to the Sultan's palace?"

"How can you do such a thing?" her sister cried. "The Sultan is a cruel old man. You'll be thrown into a foul dungeon like the others!"

"Not if you will help me with my plan," said Scheherazade. "If I succeed, I will be safe and the women of the city will be freed from the Sultan's cruelty."

"What do you wish me to do? How can I be of any help?"

"In the evening, when we are brought to the Sultan's chamber, I will ask that you be allowed to attend me." And Scheherazade told her sister what she must say.

The younger sister said, "I will do what you ask."

That evening the sister accompanied Scheherazade to the Sultan's chamber. As she helped her older sister remove her face veil and garments, she said, "Dear sister, I beg one last favor from you. Will you tell me one of your delightful stories before we part?"

Scheherazade turned to the Sultan. "Will Your Highness permit me to grant this favor?"

He nodded and belched, for he had as usual eaten too heavily. "Yes, yes. Go ahead."

So Scheherazade began a story. She told it so skillfully that the Sultan became absorbed in the story in spite of himself. Then, as the night grew late, she broke off at the most exciting part of the tale.

Yawning, she said, "I am too sleepy to remember what happens next. But I will think of it tomorrow and finish the tale tomorrow night if Your Highness wishes."

By this time the Sultan was very eager to hear the story's ending, so he agreed to this request.

The next evening, Scheherazade finished the tale and began another. Again she broke off before the end, pleading that she was too sleepy to remember the rest of the story.

"Very well, you may take your rest now," said the Sultan, quite disappointed. "Tomorrow you must try to remember the rest of the story. I want to know how it ends."

Scheherazade continued each evening in the same way. The nights of her storytelling stretched on and on and on to one thousand and one, while the townspeople rejoiced in the success of Scheherazade's efforts to save the young women of the city.

· · ·

What happened to Scheherazade after the one thousand and one tales were told?

One storyteller would have us believe that at this point Scheherazade and the wicked Sultan fell in love and lived happily ever after. Another narrator tells us that Scheherazade, having born three babies during this period, cast herself at the Sultan's feet, begging for her life for the sake of her soon-to-be-orphaned children. The Sultan, entranced by the discovery of three male heirs—which he apparently had not known about—at once became a reformed man. Repenting of his earlier cruel treatment of the other maidens, he spared our heroine's life. Needless to say, in this version they also lived happily ever after.

Those readers who can accept that the clever, courageous Scheherazade ended her days in this fashion may choose either of the above endings to the tale.

But, having been moved by Scheherazade's courage, having empathized with her revulsion and horror at the Sultan's cruelty, and having enjoyed her clever strategy to free the women of the city and to survive herself, many readers may well be disappointed with these meek and improbable endings.

Rather than force Scheherazade to change her admirable character, I would suggest another ending. Freed at this point by the Sultan's death (for I loyally believe Scheherazade could have produced another thousand tales if necessary), acclaimed by the grateful citizens of Samarkand, she did what any clever storyteller would do: Using her earlier education provided by the best tutors, she of course wrote down for posterity a more polished version of her one thousand and one tales.

BIBLIOGRAPHY

. . .

The original sources for the retold tales in this book were found for the most part in folk tale collections of the late nineteenth and early twentieth centuries: "The Maid of the North" drawn from the *Kalevala* (1907), 2 vol., William Kirby. "The Giant's Daughter" and "Finn Magic" from *Weird Tales of the Northern Seas* (1903), Jonas Lie, translated by R. Nesbit Bain. "How the Summer Queen Came to Canada" from *Canadian Wonder Tales* (1918 and 1922), Cyrus Macmillan. "Mulha" from *Fairy Tales from South Africa* (1910), Sarah Bourhill and Beatrice Drake. "The Tiger and the Jackal" from *Tales of the Punjab* (1917), Florie Annie Steele. "Maria Morevna" from *Russian Wonder Tales* (1912), Post Wheeler. "The Monkey's Heart" from *The Lilac Fairy Book* (1910), and "The Twelve Hunts-men" from *Green Fairy Book* (n.d.), both edited by Andrew Lang. "The Old Woman and Her Rice Cakes" from *Tales of Laughter* (1908), Kate D. Wiggins; this tale is also found in *Japanese Fairy Tales* (c. 1918), Lafcadio Hearn. "The Stars in the Sky" from *More English Fairy Tales* (1904), Joseph Jacobs. "The Hunter Maiden" from *Zuni Folk Tales* (1901), Frank H. Cushing. "Bending Willow" from *American Indian Fairy Tales* (1895), Margaret Compton. "Duffy and the Devil" from *Popular Romances from the West of England* (1881), Robert Hunt. "Elsa and the Evil Wizard" from *Old Swedish Fairy Tales* (1925), Anna Wahlenberg, translated by A. DeC. Patterson. "The Husband Who Stayed at Home" and "East of the Sun, West of the Moon" from *Popular Tales from the Norse* (1859), Asbjornsen and Moe, translated by G. W. Dasent.

My version of "Scheherazade Retold" is based in part on Andrew Lang's tale in *Arabian Nights* (1898). "Fair Exchange" was developed from an incident in Lady Wilde's *Ancient Legends of Ireland* (1887). Both "Gawain and the Lady Ragnell" and "Lanval and the Lady Triamor" are drawn from fourteenth- and fifteenth-century manuscript tales edited and printed in scholarly collections during the nineteenth century. A more recent edition of the tales is *Middle English Verse Romances*, Donald Sands, ed. (Holt, Rinehart and Winston, 1966).

Several thousand individual folk tales were read in a search for neglected tales of resourceful and courageous heroines to retell. My earlier collection, *Tatterhood and Other Tales* (1978), and this present book of tales are the result. In addition to public libraries and university libraries, the Reference Collection of Children's Books at the Donnell Library in New York City and the Osborne and Lillian H. Smith Collections in Toronto were very useful in researching the folk tales. I take this opportunity to express my thanks to the reference librarians in both Toronto and the New York area for their generous help in locating needed volumes.